felted
feathered friends

Techniques and Projects
for Needle-Felted Birds

Creative Publishing
international

Laurie Sharp
Photography by Kevin Sharp

Creative Publishing international

Copyright © 2012
Creative Publishing international, Inc.

First published in the United States of America by
Creative Publishing international, Inc., a member of
Quayside Publishing Group
400 First Avenue North
Suite 300
Minneapolis, MN 55401
1-800-328-3895
www.creativepub.com

Visit www.Craftside.Typepad.com for a behind-the-scenes peek at our crafty world!

ISBN: 978-1-58923-694-3

Library of Congress Cataloging-in-Publication Data

Sharp, Laurie.
  Felted feathered friends : techniques and projects for needle-felted birds / Laurie Sharp, Kevin Sharp.
      pages cm.
  Summary: "This adorable book shows how to make a wide variety of birds by needle felting—sculpting wool roving into a three-dimensional figure using a special barbed needle. Each project includes a fun photo of the project with step-by-step instructions that result in 20 types of feathered friends! With Felted Feathered Friends, you'll learn to make endearing creatures such as: – A snowy owl – A peacock – A Great Blue Heron – A bluebird – A robin – A flamingo – A pair of lovebirds – And much more. These delightful creations will put a smile on anyone's face, and with easy-to-follow directions and the author's enthusiastic and expert guidance, anyone can take part in the feathered fun!"— Provided by publisher.

  ISBN 978-1-58923-694-3 (hardback)
  1. Felt work. 2. Felting. 3. Birds in art. I. Sharp, Kevin. II. Title.

TT849.5.S525 2012
677'.63--dc23

2011046122

Photography: Kevin Sharp
Copy Editor: Catherine Broberg
Proofreader: Karen Ruth
Book Design: Judy Morgan
Page Layout: Linnea Fitzpatrick

Printed in China
10 9 8 7 6 5 4 3 2 1

contents

introduction

A Bird came down the Walk—
He did not know I saw—
He bit an Angleworm in halves
And ate the fellow, raw,

And then he drank a Dew
From a convenient Grass—
And then hopped sidewise to the Wall
To let a Beetle pass—

by Emily Dickinson

Welcome to the amazing world of needle-felted birds. As a young artist, I spent countless hours drawing the birds that visited the feeder of my home in upstate New York. In later years, after I discovered needle felting, birds resurfaced as a theme in my work. The wide variety of color, texture, and shape of birds provides endless inspiration for needle felting. I am delighted to share with you the tools, materials, and techniques so that, with a little practice and experience, you can joyfully create your own flock of woolly birds.

The materials and tools are easy to use and are readily available since needle felting is gaining in popularity as a hobby and art form. If you're just beginning to needle felt, I hope this book will lead you on your way to discovering a fun new way to make birds. For those of you with a little more experience, the techniques and patterns will help inspire you to go beyond what you may already know and try new things.

The projects in this book are organized from easy to more complicated designs. The bluebird is a great project to warm up your felting chops. Once you develop a feel for working with wool and the felting needle, try the peacock or flamingo. If you are unsure of what to do with a felted bird, the bird mobile or cake topper are great ways to showcase your craftiness and make someone smile. Most important, use this book as a guideline for developing your own techniques and style. The amazing thing about needle-felted artwork is that no one style looks the same as anyone else's. I hope you have as much fun learning to make needle-felted birds as I have in creating this book.

Happy felting!

Before you begin making needle-felted birds, there are a few materials and tools that you will need.

materials & tools

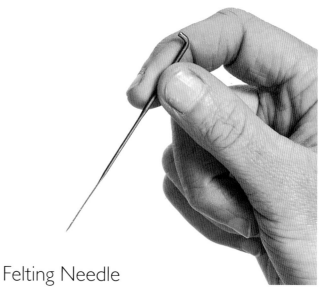

Felting Needle

The felting needle is a thin, 3" (7.5 cm) long sharp, barbed instrument used to shape and sculpt wool. Repeatedly poking a piece of wool roving with the needle will cause the fibers to bind together and felt. Felting needles come in various sizes, but for all the projects in this book, you will need a 38-gauge triangle needle. This is the most common type needle available.

Foam Pad

Since you will be repeatedly jabbing a very sharp needle into wool, you will need a soft surface to work on, such as a foam pad or sponge. The best work surface is high-density foam with a thickness of 1½" (4 cm). When your needle is not in use, keep it in a safe place. I like to push the needle deep into the side of the foam pad for storage.

Wool

Wool from a sheep is the best material to use for needle felting because wool has tiny, microscopic scales on the fiber. When the felting needle is poked into the wool, the barbs on the needle grab the scales on the wool causing them to tangle and felt.

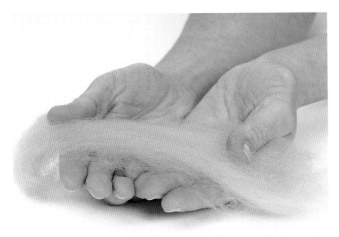

Wool is available at many yarn and fiber stores in the form of roving. Roving is wool fibers that have been combed and arranged in a long, thick rope all running in the same direction.

These are the three main tools/materials that you will use for most of the projects in this book. It is helpful to have other supplies such as sewing needles, thread, scissors, and beads to complete the projects. To make birds with legs, you will also need wire or chenille stems (pipe cleaners), wire cutters, pliers, and embroidery floss.

Sculptural needle felting involves a few easy techniques that you can master quickly with just a little practice.

basic techniques

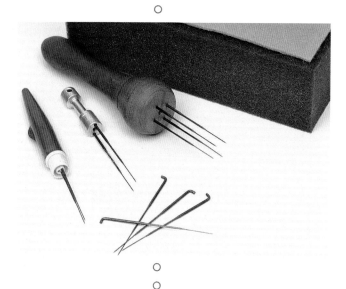

The techniques taught for making needle-felted birds are those that I have found to work best for me. As you gain experience using the felting needle and wool, you may find a different technique works better for you. Take my suggestions to get you started, but experiment yourself. There is no specific right or wrong way to needle felt.

Working with the Felting Needle

The felting needle is a very sharp instrument. When you first start out, pay close attention to where you poke the needle. Watch your fingers. If you do stab yourself, wash with soap and water to avoid any possible infection.

Obviously, this is not a craft for very young children. In general, children over the age of eight can use the felting needle safely. Adult supervision is a good idea.

Hold the needle comfortably in your hand as you would a pencil. If you have trouble gripping the needle, you can buy felting needle holders with either plastic or wooden handles.

Try not to forcefully jab the needle into your work. It will not make the job go faster and you will probably end up with a broken needle. You only need to penetrate the surface about a ¼" (6 mm) because the barbs (which do the felting work) are on the tip of the needle. You can needle in the same spot to get a deeper groove in the wool. The more you needle, the more the wool will felt and bind, and the stiffer it will become.

Working with Wool

Wool fiber that has not yet been spun into yarn is called roving. The sheep has been sheared; the wool washed, carded, dyed, and combed so that the fibers all lie in the same direction. The wool will felt better if the fibers don't all lie in the same direction as they are when processed into roving. I usually recommend that you fluff up the roving before you use it for needle felting. Take a handful of roving and pull the fibers apart, layer them on top of each other crosswise, then pull apart again. Repeat pulling apart and layering fibers until the wool seems fluffy like a cloud, not in a rope.

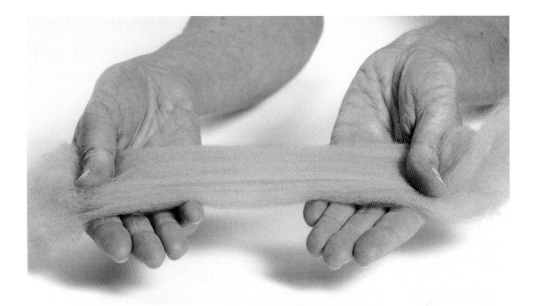

Any wool will felt, but some types felt better than other types. Experimentation is the key. I have found that coarse wool fiber, such as wool from Romney or Corriedale, needle felts better than finer wool, such as merino.

Wool is a very satisfying material to work with unless you are allergic to it. If you do have problems handling wool, you can use other

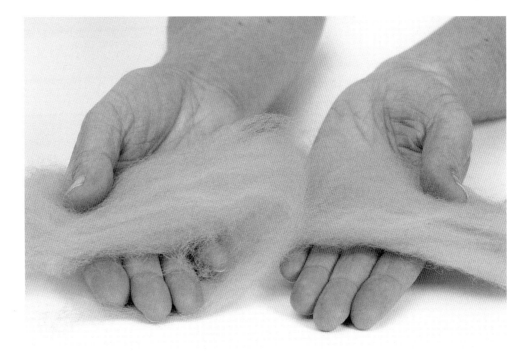

animal fibers instead, such as llama, alpaca, canine, or angora fibers.

Throughout the book, I use the term "needle" as a verb to describe the act of needle felting; that is "needle the shape all around to make it smooth." In this example, you would hold the felting needle and poke it into the wool fiber on the surface of the shape.

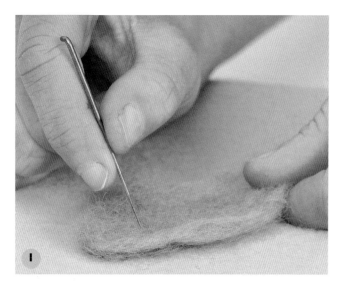

Shaping the Wool Fiber

Sculpting wool is similar to sculpting clay. Use your hands to mold, fold, flatten, and shape the wool and use the felting needle to hold the shape.

Flat pieces, such as wings and tails, are made using layered wisps of wool. The directions for each individual bird project will tell you how much wool to use, but remember, needle felting is not an exact science. Ultimately it is up to you as to how much wool to use. With practice you will get more of a feel for how much wool to use depending on the desired outcome.

Needle all over the surface of the flat piece (1). Gently lift the piece of wool off the foam pad and turn it over and needle the opposite side. Here it is important not to needle too deeply or the wool will get embedded in the foam.

To shape the piece, use the tip of your felting needle (or your fingers—but be careful of the needle) and lift the edge toward the middle and needle in place (2).

For three-dimensional shapes, the technique I use is as follows: begin with a small handful of wool. It is easier to build up a piece starting with less wool than it is to start with a bunch of wool and trying to needle it down to size. Roll the wool tightly and snugly into the shape described in the instructions for your project. Needle to hold the shape (3). Some instructions may say to needle more at one end (i.e., the tail end is narrower than the head of a bird). Here, you will use the felting needle to sculpt more deeply into the wool.

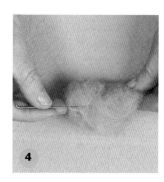

Build up the shape by adding small layers of wool to areas that you want larger. Needle between adding layers (4).

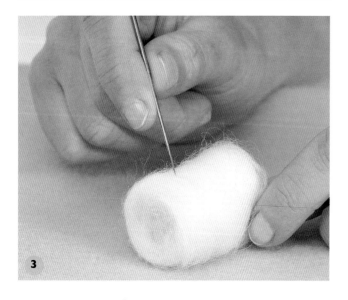

Attaching Parts

The birds in this book are similarly constructed. Make the body, built up with layers of wool. Then make other parts to proportion and add on. Often in the instructions you will see the phrase "keep the fibers loose at one end." This means that it is much easier to attach felted parts together if some of the wool has been left loose, thus enabling the fibers from one piece to bind into the fibers of another. It is harder to attach two pieces together that are both well felted with no loose "grabby" parts.

A note about bird legs. I would recommend getting your felting fingers warmed up by making birds without legs to start. Wool is very light and it can be difficult to get sculptures to stand on their own or even with the help of wire legs. Some of the projects will show you how to make birds with legs but getting the bird to balance can be a bit tricky. Remember to be patient and practice.

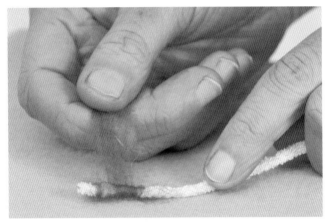

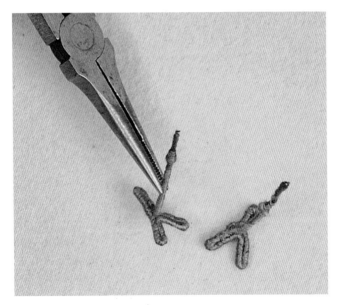

Experiment with different types of wire—you can use chenille stems, cloth-covered florist wire, bare wire, baling wire, anything that works. Wrap the wire with six-strand embroidery floss or wool roving. A touch of glue helps keep the floss or wool in place. Beginning with chenille stems is good because the wool fiber or floss will have something to grab to help it stay in place.

Here too you will need patience and practice. It is most important to wrap evenly and tightly.

I usually wrap the wire first, then bend the claws or toes into place using needle-nose pliers. It often seems more difficult to wrap the claws after they have been bent, but try both ways and see what works best for you.

Well, I think I've covered everything to start. Ready to fly? Here we go.

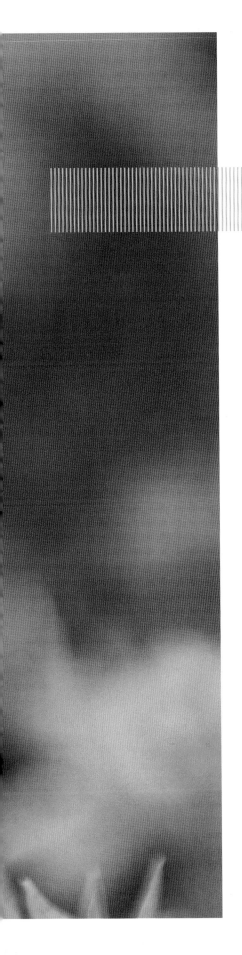

bluebird

This pattern will show you the basic steps in making a needle-felted bird. It is easy to modify this basic shape to use for making other kinds of birds. Use yellow wool to make a goldfinch, or a darker, bolder blue to make a painted bunting.

MATERIALS

- ½ oz. (14 g) blue wool roving
- small amount of yellow wool roving
- foam pad
- scissors
- needle and thread
- black beads for eyes
- ruler
- felting needle

BODY

1. Measure a 5" × 3" (12.5 × 7.5 cm) piece of blue wool. Roll tightly and shape into a 2" (5 cm)-long crescent shape. The middle should be wider than the ends.

2. Needle all over the body to help hold the shape.

TAIL

3. Choose one end to be the tail and needle it to a flat point. Wrap a wisp of blue wool around the tail end and needle to help build up the tail.

HEAD

4. The opposite end will be the head of the bluebird. Wrap layers of blue wool around the head end to help build it up and shape it. Continue to add small wisps of blue wool all over the body of the bluebird until you are satisfied with the size. Needle to help hold the shape.

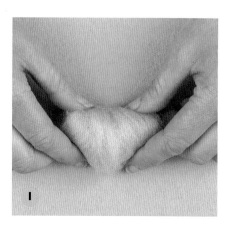
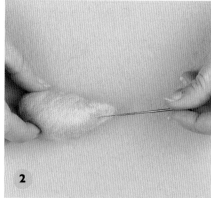
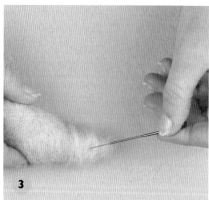
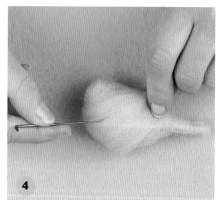

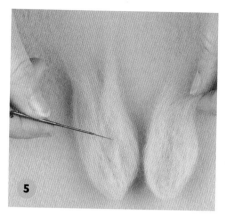

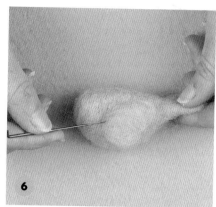

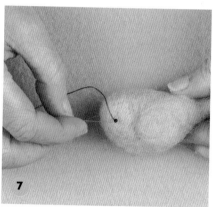

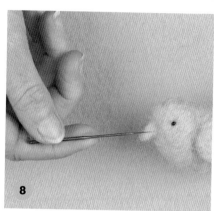

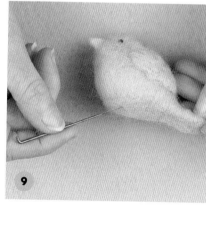

WINGS

5. Measure a 2" (5 cm) piece of blue wool, fold it in half, and needle the surface flat. Turn the wing over and needle the opposite side. Keep the fibers loose at one end to help attach the wing to the body. Make two wings.

6. Position the wings on the body and needle the loose fibers from the wing into the body to attach.

EYES AND BEAK

7. To attach the beads for eyes, thread a needle and bring it from one side of the head through to the other side. Don't pull the thread all the way through. Place a bead on the needle and insert the needle back through the head to the other side. Thread another bead on the needle and sew back through the head again. Sew back and forth a few times to secure the beads to the head.

8. Fold a wisp of yellow wool into a triangle shape and needle. Position the beak on the front of the bluebird's face and needle to attach.

9. Needle the base of the bird flat so that the bird can balance.

cardinal

The male northern cardinal is uniquely colored red. The female is a buff-brown color with a reddish tinge on wings, tail, and crest. A bright red cardinal hanging in a tree looks festive during the holidays. Use this same pattern for other crested birds, such as blue jays and cedar waxwings.

MATERIALS

- ½ oz. (14 g) red wool
- small amount of black and orange wool
- felting needle
- wooden skewer
- foam pad
- scissors
- needle and thread
- black beads for eyes
- ruler
- ribbon

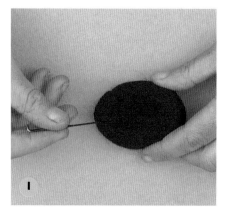

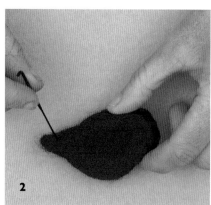

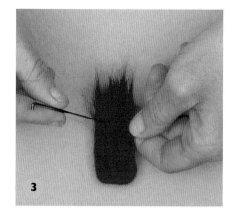

BODY

1. Measure a 10" x 3" (25.5 x 7.5 cm) piece of red wool. Roll tightly and shape into a 2½" (6.5 cm) oval shape. Needle all over the body to help hold the shape.

2. Build up the bird by wrapping layers of red wool all around the body; wrap evenly and firmly. Needle the surface smooth. Needle one end of the oval narrower. This is where the tail will be attached.

TAIL

3. Measure a 2½" (6.5 cm) piece of red wool and fold in half. Needle the surface flat. Turn the piece over and needle the opposite side. Pick up and needle the fibers to form a straight edge along the bottom. Leave the fibers loose at the other end to help attach the tail to the body.

4. Position the tail on the back of the cardinal's body and needle loose fibers from the tail into the body to help attach smoothly.

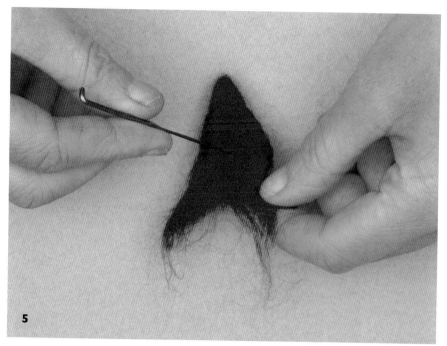

HEAD

5. Use the skewer to help roll a 3" × 1½" (7.5 × 4 cm) piece of red wool into a 1½" (4 cm) tall cone. Needle the surface to help hold the shape. Keep the fibers loose at the wider end of the cone.

6. Position the wide end of the cone on the top front of the cardinal and needle the loose fibers into the body.

7. Wrap several wisps of red wool around the area of attachment and needle smooth.

(continued)

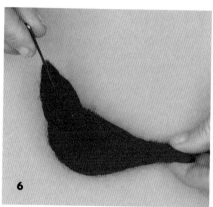

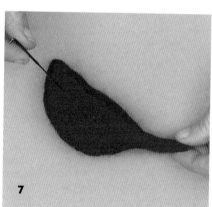

BEAK AND FACE MARKINGS

8. Use the skewer to roll a wisp of orange wool into a small cone shape. Keep the fibers loose at one end to help attach the beak to the head.

9. Position the beak and needle to attach.

10. Needle a band of black wool around the beak.

11. Sew black beads on each side of the cardinal's head for eyes.

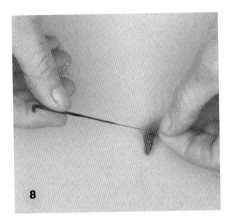

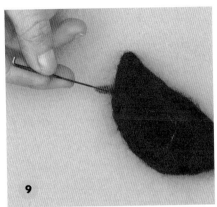

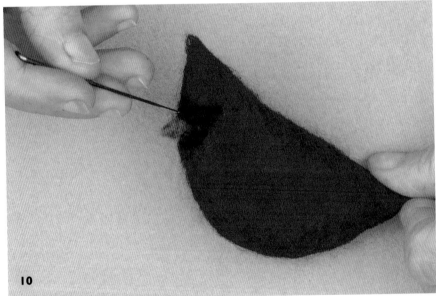

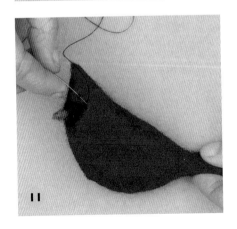

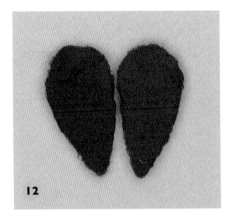

12

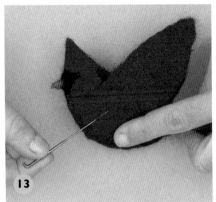

13

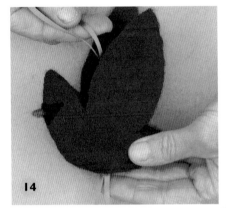

14

WINGS

12. Measure a 4" × 2" (10 × 5 cm) piece of red wool and arrange the fibers in a fan shape. Needle the surface. Turn the wing over and needle the opposite side. Lift up the fibers from the edge and needle them toward the middle to shape the wing. Make two wings.

13. Position the wings on the side of the cardinal's body and needle to attach.

14. Sew a ribbon through the cardinal's body, hang him up, and enjoy your beautiful handwork!

dove

To the Egyptians, doves are a symbol of peace and quiet innocence. In some Asian cultures, the dove symbolizes peace and longevity. This needle-felted version is easy to make. It is helpful to remember that the size of the dove's head is small in proportion to the rest of the bird's body and the shape of the dove's body is rounder than other birds.

MATERIALS

- ½ oz. (14 g) white wool
- small amount of black and yellow wool
- felting needle
- foam pad

- scissors
- needle and thread
- black beads for eyes
- ruler
- ribbon

BODY

1. Measure a 10" × 3" (25 × 7.5 cm) piece of white wool. Roll tightly and shape into a 2" (5 cm)-wide ball. Needle all over the body to help hold the shape.

2. Build up the body by wrapping layers of white wool all around the body. Wrap evenly and firmly. Needle the surface smooth.

HEAD

3. Measure a 6" × 2" (15 × 5 cm) piece of white wool and roll into a 1½" (4 cm)-wide ball. Needle the surface to help hold the shape.

4. Position the head on top of the body and needle to attach.

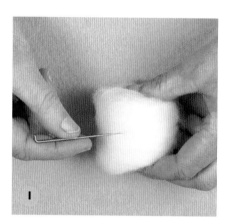
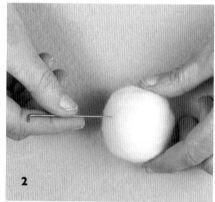
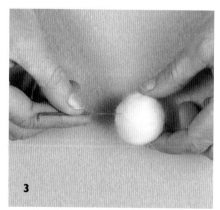

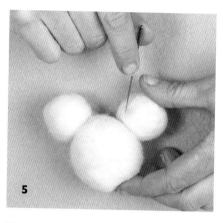

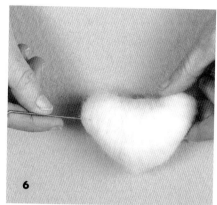

5. Make another white ball the same size as the head and needle to the back of the dove's body, opposite the head. This shape will help form the bird's body.

6. Build up the whole shape by wrapping layers of white wool all around the body and head. Needle between layers to help smooth and shape the wool.

TAIL

7. Layer several wisps of white wool on the foam pad in a triangle shape that measures 3" (7.5 cm) along each side. Needle the surface, turn the piece over and needle the other side.

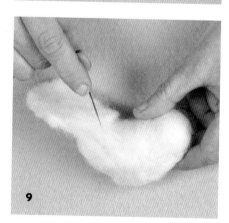

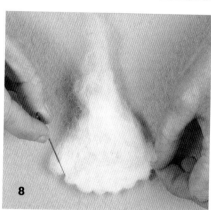

8. Use the felting needle to shape the wool on the base of the triangle into a scalloped edge. Leave the fibers loose at the opposite point to help attach the tail to the body.

9. Position the tail on the back end of the dove and needle to attach.

10. Needle layers of white wool all around the tail and body to help smooth the area of attachment.

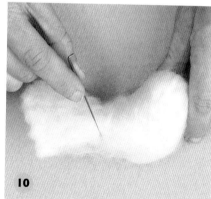

(continued)

WINGS

11. Measure three 4" × 1" (10 × 2.5 cm) strips of white wool and arrange in a fan shape, overlapping the wool. Needle the surface. Gently lift the wing off the foam pad and needle the opposite side. Each wing should measure about 5" × 4" (12.5 × 10 cm) and have a thickness of approximately ¼" (6 mm).

12. Needle a scallop pattern along the top edge of the wing. Use the felting needle to pick up wool from the sides and needle toward the middle.

13. Make two wings.

14. Position the wings on each side of the dove's body and needle to attach.

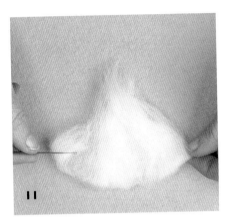

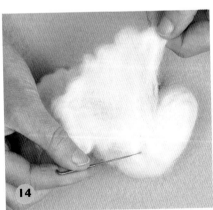

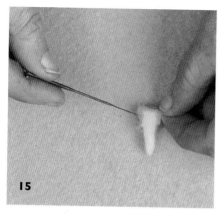

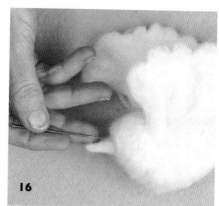

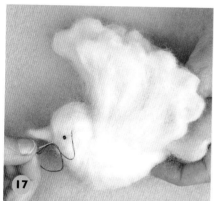

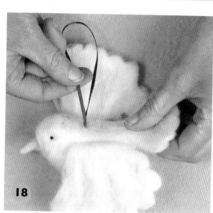

BEAK AND EYES

15. Needle a wisp of yellow wool into a ½" (1 cm) cone shape. Leave the fibers loose at one end to help attach the beak to the dove's face.

16. Position the beak on the dove and needle the loose fibers from the beak into the dove's head.

17. Sew black beads on each side of the dove's head for eyes.

18. Sew a piece of ribbon through the dove's body to hang and enjoy.

nesting robin

Robins are distinctive, potbellied birds who have adapted well to urban habitats. The female robin is a lighter gray than the male. This sweet little robin and her nest of pretty blue eggs is the perfect decoration for a spring table. Use a nice branch or piece of driftwood as a base for the robin and her nest.

MATERIALS

- ½ oz. (14 g) dark brown wool
- ⅕ oz. (6 g) brown wool
- small amount of black, white, yellow, and copper wool
- ⅕ oz. (6 g) light blue wool
- felting needle
- wooden skewer
- foam pad
- scissors
- needle and thread
- ruler
- branch or piece of driftwood
- glue

BODY

1. Measure a 10" × 3" (25 × 7.5 cm) piece of dark brown wool. Roll tightly and shape into a 2½" (6.5 cm)-long crescent. Needle all over the body to help hold the shape.

2. Gently pull some wool loose from one end of the body. Needle the loose wool so that the body tapers toward the tail. Needle to help hold the shape. Shape the opposite end so it is rounded and smooth.

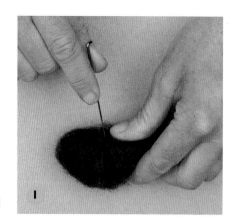

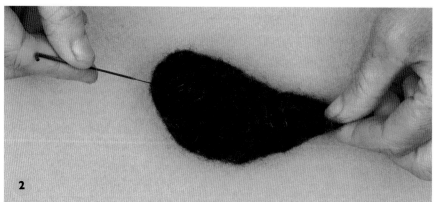

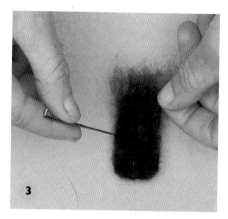

3

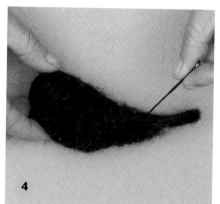

4

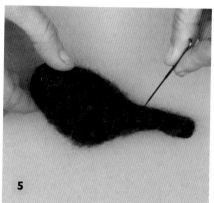

5

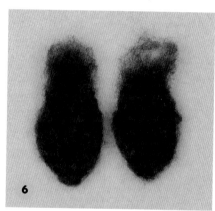

6

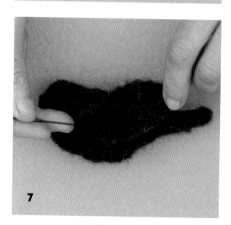

7

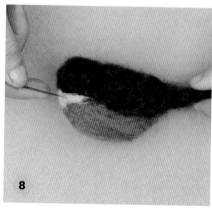

8

TAIL

Measure a 4" × 1" (10 × 2.5 cm) piece of dark brown wool and fold it in half. Needle the piece into a 2" (5 cm) rectangle. Keep the fibers loose at one end to help attach the tail to the body.

Position the tail on the body and needle to attach.

Needle a few layers of dark brown wool all over the body to help build the shape.

WINGS

Measure a 5" × 2" (12.5 × 5 cm) piece of dark brown wool. Fold in half and needle the surface. Use the felting needle to lift the sides of the wing toward the middle to help shape. Make two wings.

Position the wings on the robin and needle to attach.

MARKINGS

Needle several wisps of copper wool on the robin's breast. Needle a patch of white wool on the robin's throat.

(continued)

EYES

9. Needle a wisp of white wool into a circle on each side of the robin's head. Needle a smaller circle of black wool inside the white circle. Needle a speck of white wool inside the black.

BEAK

10. Use the skewer to help roll a wisp of yellow wool into a cone shape. Slide the wool off the skewer and needle to help hold the shape. Leave the fibers loose at one end to help attach the beak to the head.

11. Position the beak on the robin and needle to attach.

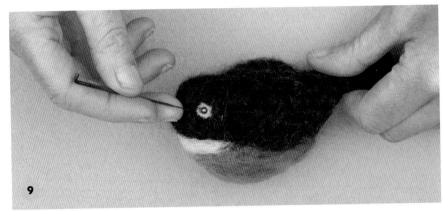

9

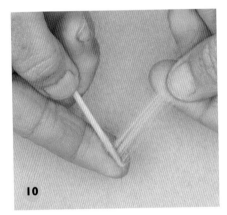

10

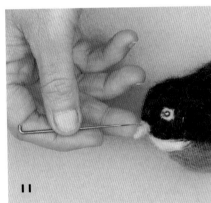

11

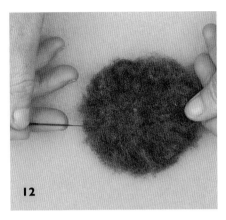

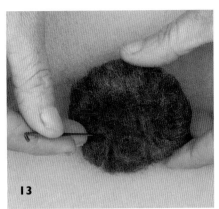

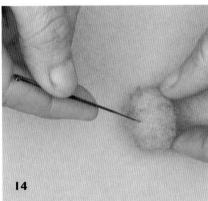

NEST

12. Arrange several layers of light brown wool into a 4" (10 cm) wide circle. Needle the surface lightly. Turn the circle over and needle the opposite side. Needle deep in the middle of the circle to help form a bowl/nest shape.

13. Use the felting needle to pick up the sides and needle toward the middle.

EGGS

14. Roll a thin strip of blue wool into an oval shape. Needle to help the egg hold shape.

15. Glue the nest to a piece of driftwood. Place the robin next to the nest and find a nice window to display.

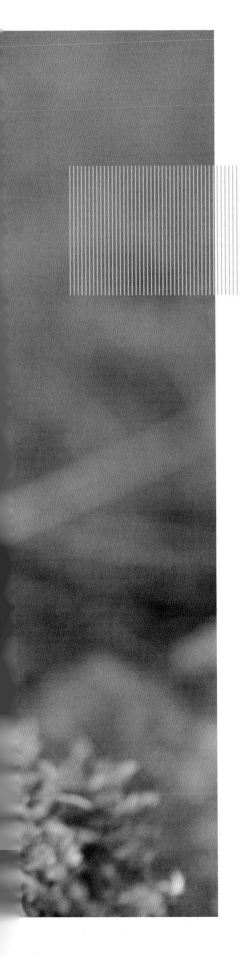

swan and cygnet

Most elegant of all waterfowl, the swan is all grace and beauty. The gray cygnet sits comfortably on her back, enjoying the ride. Needle felt an oval base of blue or green wool so the swan and cygnet will have a pond to swim in.

MATERIALS

- ½ oz. (14 g) white wool
- ⅕ oz. (6 g) gray wool
- small amount of black wool
- felting needle
- wooden skewer
- foam pad
- scissors
- needle and thread
- black beads for eyes
- ruler

SWAN BODY

1. Measure a 7" × 3" (18 × 7.5 cm) piece of white wool. Roll tightly into a 3" × 1½" (7.5 × 4 cm) barrel shape. Needle the surface to help hold the shape.

2. Needle one end into a narrow point for the tail. Add another layer of white wool around the body and needle to smooth the surface.

3. Needle several layers of white wool to the breast.

4. Needle a slight indentation on the top front of the swan's body. This is where the neck will be attached to the body. Set the body aside for now.

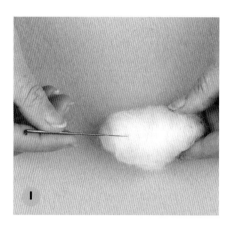

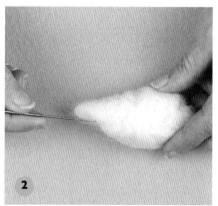

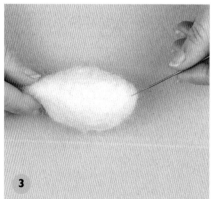

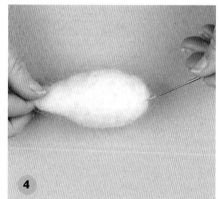

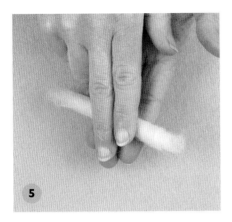

NECK AND HEAD

5. Measure a 5" × 1" (12.5 × 2.5 cm) piece of white wool and use the wooden skewer to tightly roll it into a 3" (7.5 cm)-long neck. Needle the surface to hold the roll together. Keep the fibers loose at one end to help attach the neck to the body. Roll around in your hands to help shape the neck and make it slender.

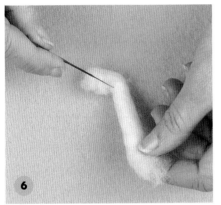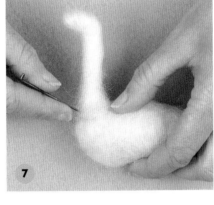

HEAD

6. Bend the top ½" (1 cm) of the neck and needle an indent. This will be the swan's head.

7. Position the neck on top of the body and needle to attach. Needle all around the area of attachment. Add wisps of wool around the neck to help build up the shape.

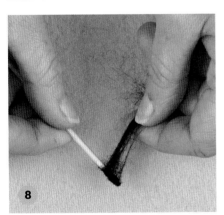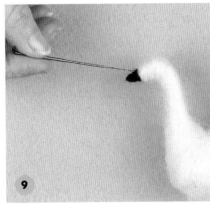

BEAK

8. Use the wooden skewer to help roll a wisp of black wool into a tube shape. Slide the wool off the skewer and needle to help hold the shape. Leave the fibers loose at one end to help attach the beak to the head.

9. Position the beak on the front of the swan's head and needle to attach. Needle a strip of black wool around the area of attachment.

(continued)

EYES

10. Sew black beads on each side of
the swan's head for eyes.

WINGS

11. Measure a 4" × 1" (10 × 2.5 cm)
piece of white wool. Fold the wool
in half and needle into a V-shaped
wing. Needle the tip of the wing to
a point and leave the fibers loose at
the end of the wing to help attach
it to the body. Make two wings.

12. Position the wings on each side
of the swan's body and needle
to attach.

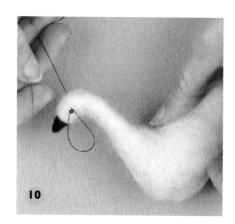

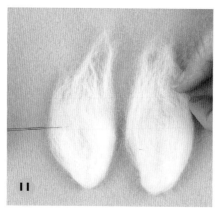

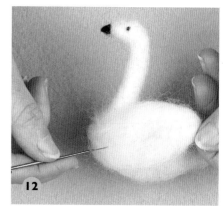

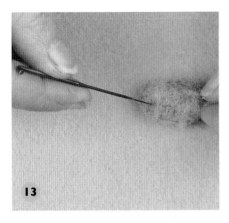

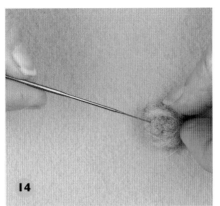

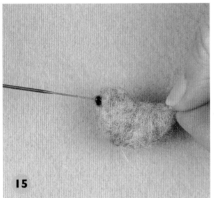

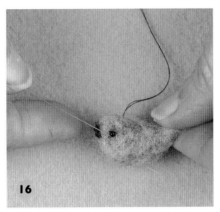

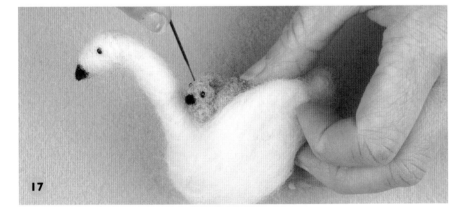

CYGNET

13. Roll a 3" (7.6 cm)-long piece of gray wool into an oval shape that measures approximately 1" (2.5 cm) long. Needle the surface to keep the wool from unrolling.

14. Roll a wisp of gray wool into a ball and needle to the body for a head.

15. Needle a wisp of black wool on the cygnet's face for a beak.

16. Sew black beads onto each side of the cygnet's head for eyes.

17. Needle the cygnet to the back of the swan between the wings.

snowy owl

Following these instructions will help you make an owl facing sideways with a turned head, but you can make one facing forward quite easily. To make a folksy-looking owl, use wool roving dyed in bright, bold colors and needle felt designs in contrasting colors on the owl's body. This owl can be simply made with plain white wings, or you can use black wool and needle a feather design. Use photographs or real snowy owls to help give you ideas for patterns.

MATERIALS

- ½ oz. (14 g) white wool
- ⅕ oz. (6 g) gray wool
- small amount of black and gold wool
- felting needle
- foam pad

- scissors
- needle and thread
- darning needle
- ruler
- scissors

BODY

1. Measure a 7" x 3" (18 x 7.5 cm) piece of white wool. Roll tightly into a 2½" (6.5 cm)-tall barrel shape with a base slightly wider than the top. The owl's head will be made separately and attached to the top of the body. Needle the surface to help hold the shape.

2. Use a darning needle to pull some wool from one side of the base, and needle to help shape the tail. Needle an indentation on the chest and stomach of the owl to help shape the body into a wedge. Needle the surface to help hold the shape.

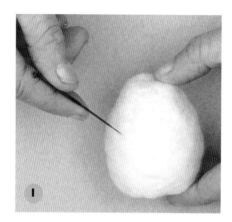

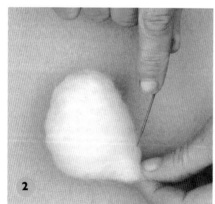

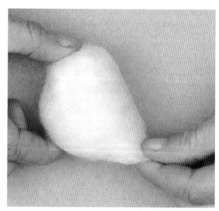

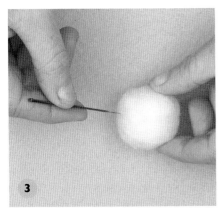

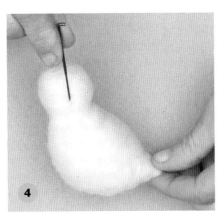

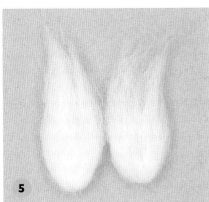

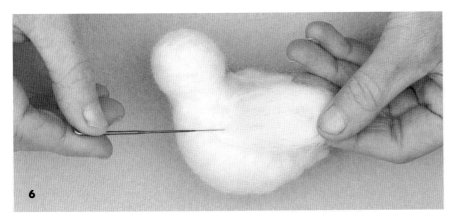

HEAD

3. Measure a 5" x 2" (12.5 x 5 cm) piece of white wool and tightly roll it into a 1½" (4 cm)-round ball. Needle the surface to hold the roll together. Roll around in your hands to make it smooth.

4. Position the head on the top of the body and needle all around the edge of the head into the body to attach.

WINGS

5. Measure a 4" x 1" (10 x 2.5 cm) piece of white wool and fold in half. Needle into a flat, oval shape. Needle the folded end into a point and keep the fibers loose at the opposite end to help attach the wing to the body. Make two wings.

6. Position the wings on the side of the owl and needle the loose fibers from the wings into the body.

(continued)

FEET

7. Measure a 3" × 2" (7.5 × 5 cm) piece of white wool and fold into a triangle. Needle the surface to help hold the shape. Choose one point of the triangle to be the back claw and the opposite side will be separated into three front claws. Needle the back claw into a narrow shape and divide the opposite side into three sections. Needle in between each section.

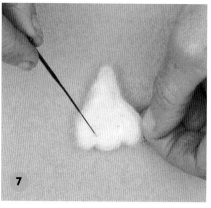

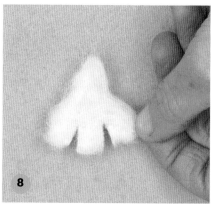

8. Use a sharp, pointed pair of scissors to snip between the front claws. Needle each claw separately to help define the shape.

9. Repeat steps 7 and 8 for the second foot.

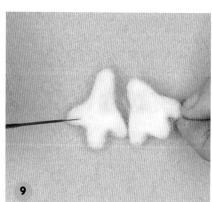

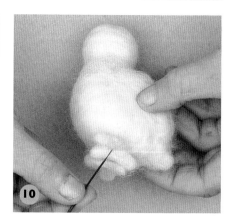

10. Position the feet on the base of the owl and needle to attach. Check to make sure that the feet are evenly spaced and the owl is balanced.

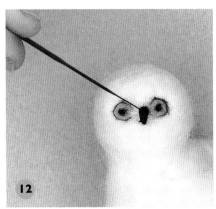

EYES AND BEAK

11. Needle two indentations on the owl's face for eyes. Needle a wisp of yellow wool into a circle in each eye. Needle a smaller wisp of black wool into the middle of the yellow. Needle a thin wisp of black wool all around the outside of the owl's eyes.

12. Needle a wisp of black wool between the eyes into a triangle shape for the beak.

yellow warbler

One of the distinguishing features of the yellow warbler is the bright yellow color of the bird's feathers. Choose the brightest yellow wool that you can find to make this bird. Or, dye plain white wool using lemon (or yellow) unsweetened powdered drink mix and water.

MATERIALS

- $\frac{3}{10}$ oz. (8.5 g) bright yellow wool
- small amount of black and light brown wool
- felting needle
- foam pad
- one 18" (45.5 cm) piece of 20-gauge cloth-covered florist wire
- wire cutters
- needle-nose pliers
- sewing needle
- thread
- black beads for eyes

BODY

1. Measure a 10" × 2" (25 × 5 cm) piece of yellow wool. Roll tightly and shape into a 2" (5 cm)-long crescent shape. Needle all over the body to help hold the shape.

2. Gently pull some wool loose from one end of the body. Needle the loose wool so that the body tapers toward the tail. Needle to help hold the shape. Shape the opposite end so it is rounded and smooth.

TAIL

3. Measure a 2" × 1" (5 × 2.5 cm) piece of yellow wool and fold it in half. Needle the piece into a 1" (2.5 cm) rectangle. Keep the fibers loose at one end to help attach the tail to the body.

4. Position the tail on the body and needle to attach. Needle a few layers of yellow wool all over the body to help build the shape.

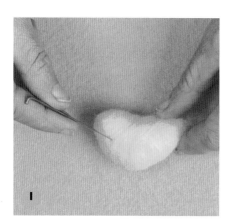

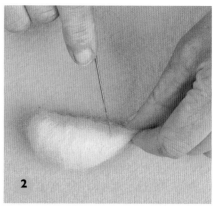

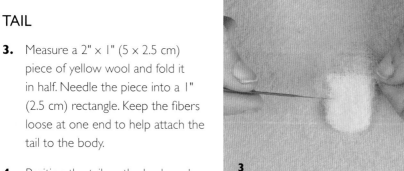

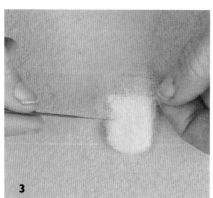

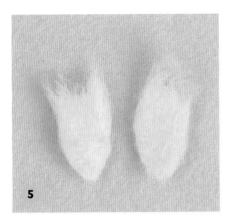

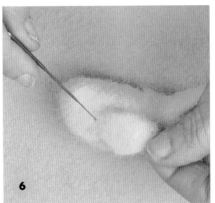

WINGS

5. Measure a 1" (2.5 cm) piece of yellow wool, fold it in half and needle the surface flat. Turn the wing over and needle the opposite side. Keep the fibers loose at one end to help attach the wing to the body. Make two wings.

6. Position the wings on the body and needle the loose fibers from the wing into the body to attach.

EYES AND BEAK

7. To attach the beads for eyes, thread a needle and pull it through from one side of the head to the other. Don't pull the thread all the way through. Place a bead on the needle and insert the needle back through the head to the other side. Thread another bead on the needle and sew back through the head again. To secure the beads, sew back and forth a few more times.

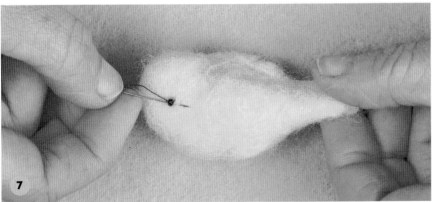

8. Fold a wisp of brown wool into a triangle shape and needle. Position the beak on the front of the warbler's face and needle to attach.

(continued)

MARKINGS

9. Needle a few wisps of light brown wool to the chest of the bird.

LEGS AND FEET

10. Cut the cloth-covered florist wire stem into two 4" (10 cm) pieces. Wrap each piece of wire with brown embroidery floss.

11. Use pliers to make five bends in the stem. Pinch the bends to make three claws.

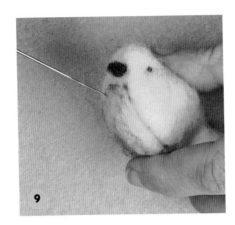

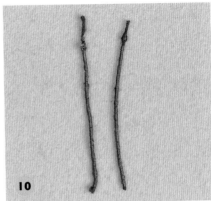

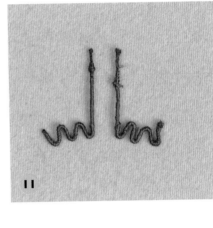

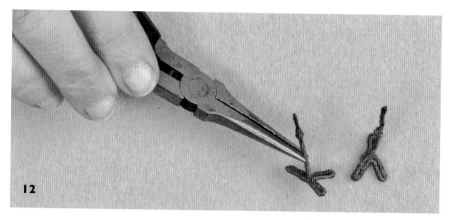

12. Twist the claws to make a foot shape and bend the wire at a right angle to the foot to make the leg piece.

13. Use the darning needle to poke two holes in the wool at the base of the warbler where the legs will be inserted.

14. Twist the end of the wire up into the warbler's body. Repeat with the opposite leg.

15. Wrap a wisp of yellow wool around the area where the wire meets the body and needle to help fix the leg into place.

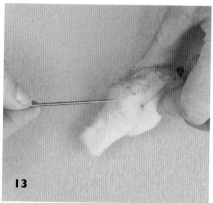

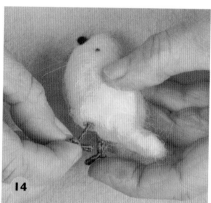

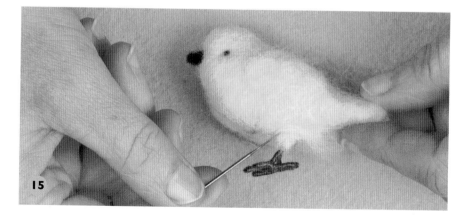

peacock

This needle-felted peacock is easier to make than it looks. You can try your hand at making a plain, white female peacock before you attempt the more colorful male. The pattern for this peacock has a simple design for the tail feather markings. Be creative and try a different design with more spots and different colors.

MATERIALS

- ½ oz. (14 g) blue wool
- ⅕ oz. (6 g) green wool
- small amount of light blue, yellow, and dark green wool
- felting needle
- foam pad
- scissors
- needle and thread
- black beads for eyes
- ruler
- mini wooden spool
- wooden skewer

BODY

1. Measure a 7" × 3" (18 × 7.5 cm) piece of blue wool. Roll tightly into a 3" × 1½" (7.5 × 4 cm) crescent shape. Needle the surface to help hold the shape.

2. Wrap the body with layers of blue wool. Needle between the layers to help build the shape. Choose which end will be the tail and needle into a flat point.

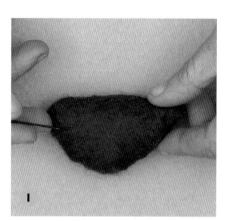

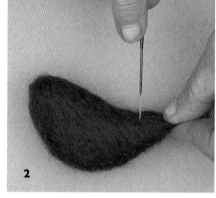

NECK

3. Measure a 5" × 1" (12.5 × 2.5 cm) piece of blue wool and use the wooden skewer to tightly roll it into a 3" (7.5 cm)-long neck. Needle the surface to hold the roll together. Keep the fibers loose at one end to help attach the neck to the body. Roll around in your hands to help shape the neck and make it slender.

4. Position the neck on top of the body and needle to attach. Needle all around the area of attachment. Add wisps of blue wool around the neck to help build up the shape.

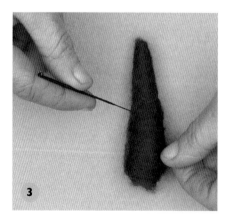

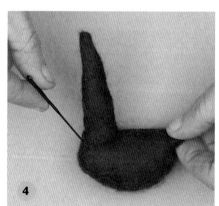

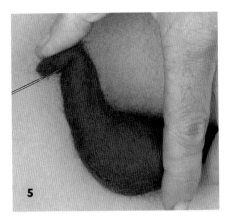

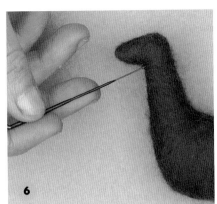

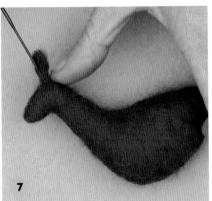

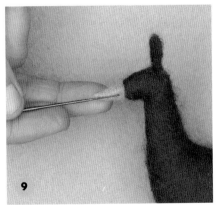

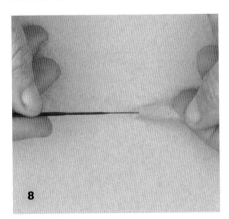

HEAD

5. Bend the top ½" (1 cm) of the neck and needle an indent. This will be the peacock's head.

6. Wrap additional blue wool around the head and needle into a cone shape.

7. To make the crown feathers, needle a wisp of blue wool into a flat fan shape and attach to the top of the peacock's head.

BEAK

8. Use the wooden skewer to help roll a wisp of yellow wool into a triangle shape. Slide the wool off the skewer and needle to help hold the shape. Leave the fibers loose at one end to help attach the beak to the head.

9. Position the beak on the front of the peacock's head and needle to attach. Needle a strip of yellow wool around the area of attachment.

(continued)

EYES

10. Sew black beads on each side of the peacock's head for eyes.

TAIL

11. Measure three 4" × 1" (10 × 2.5 cm) strips of green wool and arrange in a fan shape, overlapping the wool. Needle the surface. Gently lift the tail off the foam pad and needle the opposite side. The tail should measure about 5" × 4" (12.5 × 10 cm) and be approximately ¼" (6 mm) thick.

12. Needle a scallop pattern along the top edge of the tail. Use the felting needle to pick wool up from the sides and needle toward the middle. Make seven evenly spaced scallops. You now have seven tail sections.

13. Within each section, needle a wisp of blue wool into a circle.

14. Needle a wisp of light blue wool around each blue spot.

15. Needle a wisp of yellow wool around the light blue wool.

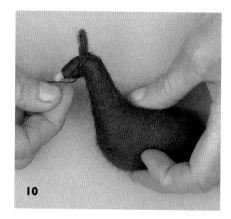

10

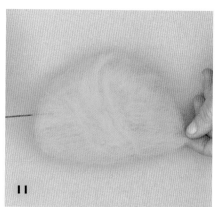

11

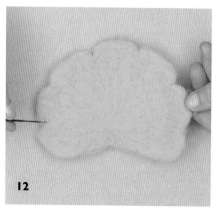

12

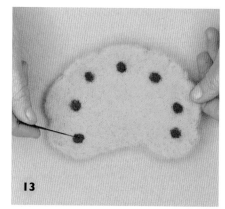

13

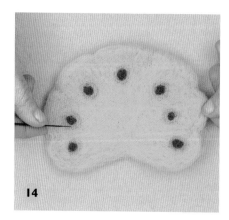

14

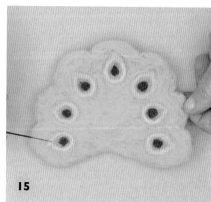

15

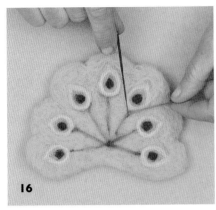

16. Use thin wisps of dark green wool to indicate feathers in each tail section. This can be as simple or intricate as you wish.

17. Needle to attach the completed tailpiece onto the middle of the peacock's back.

18. Glue the base of the peacock to the wooden spool. Make sure that it is balanced before gluing.

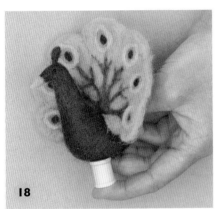

flamingo

Fun and funky, this flamingo is made with a wire armature and can be posed in many different ways. Have fun and use your sense of humor to give your flamingo some personality. You may need to practice wrapping the wire a few times if you are having difficulties making the legs.

MATERIALS

- ³⁄₁₀ oz. (8.5 g) pink wool
- small amount of black and white wool
- felting needle
- foam pad
- one 18" (45.5 cm) piece of 20-gauge cloth-covered florist wire
- wire cutters
- needle-nose pliers
- sewing needle
- thread
- black beads for eyes

WIRE ARMATURE

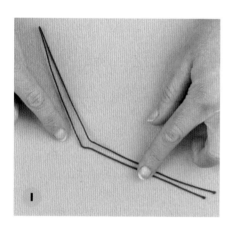 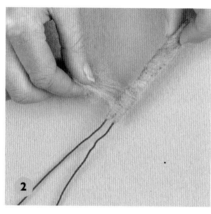

1. Bend the 18" (45.5 cm) piece of florist wire in half. Pinch the wire tightly at the bend. Then fold in half again, mark this spot and unfold. You should have a piece of wire bent in half with a mark halfway up the wire. The bottom half of the wire will be used to make the legs, and the top half will be wrapped together to make the body, neck, and head of the flamingo.

2. Tightly wrap pink wool around the top half of the bent wire. Hold the two sides of the bent wire together as you wrap the wool to the halfway mark.

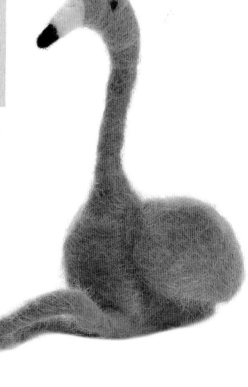

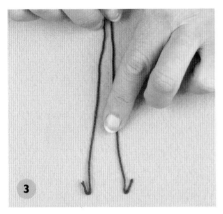

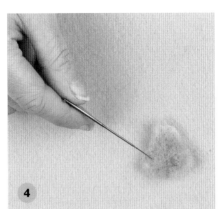

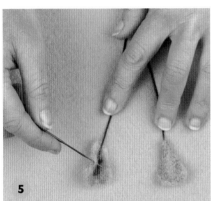

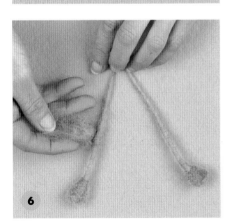

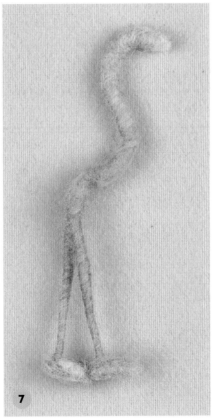

LEGS AND FEET

3. Measure 1" (2.5 cm) up from the bottom of the wire and bend in half to make a foot.

4. Needle a wisp of pink wool into a triangle shape that measures 1" (2.5 cm) on each side.

5. Place the bent wire on top of the triangle and needle the wool around the foot. Use the felting needle to lift the sides toward the middle and needle into a foot shape. Repeat steps 3 and 4 to make the other foot.

6. Wrap the wire legs with pink wool. It is best to wrap evenly with small amounts of wool.

7. Use the needle-nose pliers to bend the wire armature to define the head, neck, and body.

(continued)

BODY

8. Wrap the middle of the flamingo's body with layers of pink wool. Needle into shape. Add more wool to the breast and tail area.

9. Wrap layers of pink wool around the neck and head. Wrap more wool around the head. Needle the layers of wool around the wire.

BEAK

10. Needle a wisp of white wool into a ½" (1 cm) cone. Leave the fiber loose at the wide end.

11. Position the beak on the top of the flamingo and needle the loose fibers of the beak into the head to attach.

12. Wrap a wisp of black wool around the tip of the beak. Needle to attach.

13. Sew black beads on each side of the flamingo's head for eyes.

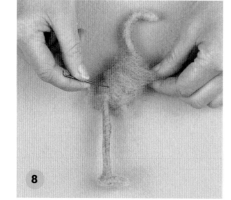

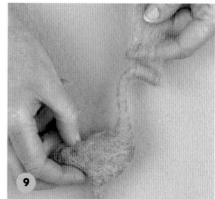

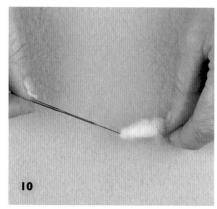

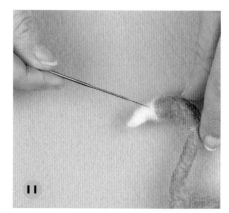

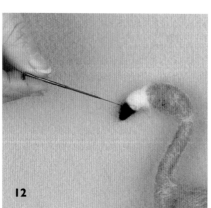

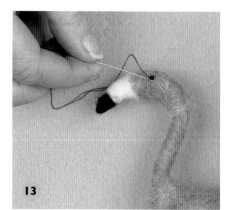

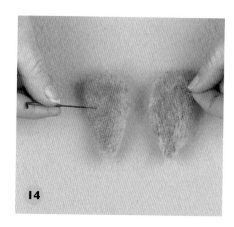

14

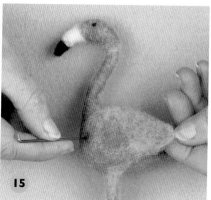

15

WINGS

14. Fold a 2" (5 cm) piece of pink wool in half. Needle the surface. Turn the wing over and use the felting needle to lift the wool from the edge toward the middle to help shape into a wing. Needle the surface.

15. Position the wings on each side of the flamingo's body and needle to attach.

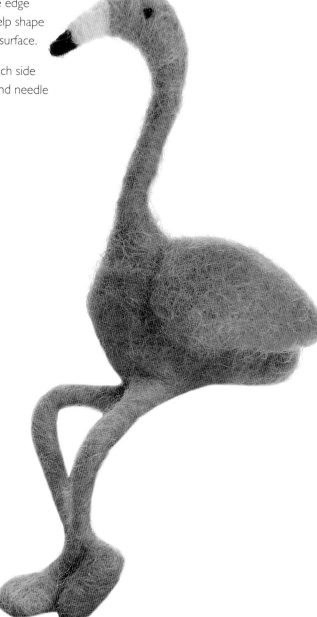

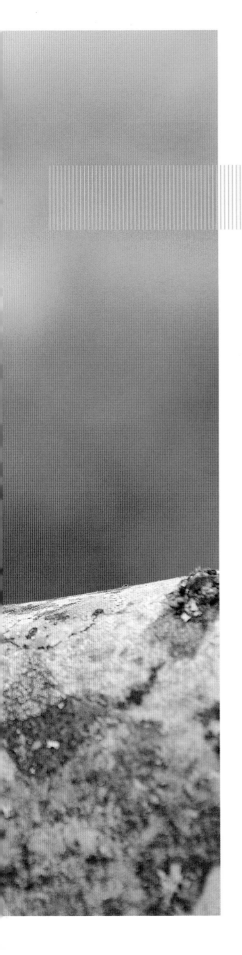

nuthatch

Nuthatches are often seen climbing trees looking for insects and seeds to eat. Blend blue and gray wool roving to get a nice blue/gray color for the wings and tail. Use two parts gray to one part blue wool and add more blue gradually blending the colors together until you have the perfect shade.

MATERIALS

- ³⁄₁₀ oz. (8.5 g) white wool
- small amount of black, blue, light brown, and gray wool
- felting needle
- one 18" (45.5 cm) piece of 20-gauge cloth-covered florist wire
- foam pad
- wire cutters
- needle-nose pliers
- sewing needle
- beads for eyes

BODY

1. Measure a 12" × 3" (30.5 × 7.5 cm) piece of white wool. Roll into a 2" (5 cm)-tall cone shape. The base of the cone should measure 1½" (4 cm) wide. Needle to help hold the fibers in place.

2. At one corner of the base, pull some wool loose and needle flat to make the tail.

3. At the top end of the cone, needle the wool into a rounded head shape. Needle at the base of the cone opposite the tail to help form the breast area. Needle and shape the wool until the body is firmly felted.

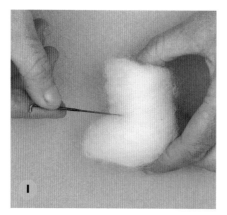

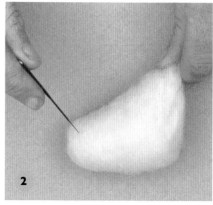

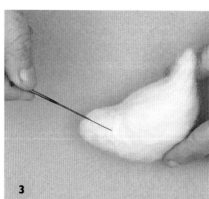

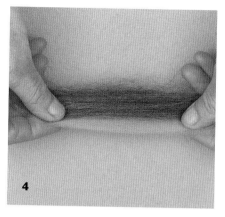

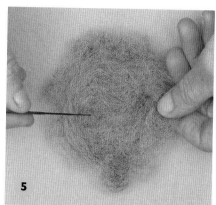

WINGS AND TAIL

The wings and tail are made in one piece and attached to the bird's body.

4. Use your fingers to blend gray wool with blue wool. Layer the wool and needle into a 3" (7.5 cm)-long flat oval shape. Pick up the piece and needle the other side flat.

5. Use the felting needle to lift up and needle the sides toward the middle to help shape the wings and tail.

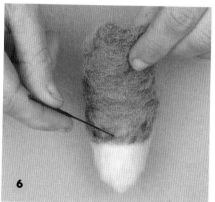

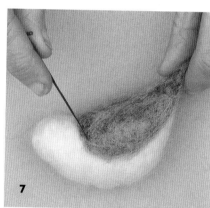

6. Position the wing and tail piece on the back of the nuthatch and needle to attach.

7. The tail should extend past the body.

8. Needle layers of light brown wool to the breast of the bird.

(continued)

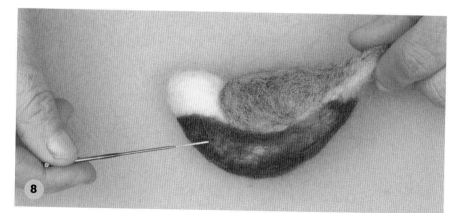

BEAK AND EYE MARKINGS

9. Needle a wisp of black wool into a tiny cone. Position the beak on the front of the bird and needle into place.

10. Add wisps of black wool and needle the eye and crown markings.

11. Sew black beads on for eyes.

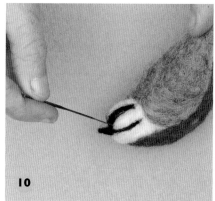

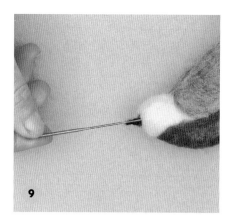

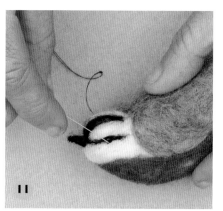

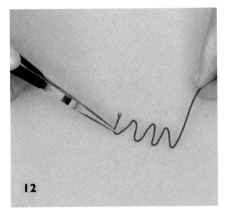

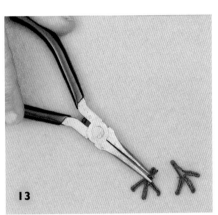

FEET AND LEGS

12. Cut two 6" (15 cm) pieces of cloth-covered florist wire. Bend into a zig-zag shape with four points.

13. Use the needle-nose pliers to bend and pinch the wire into three front claws and one back claw.

14. Twist the legs into the body. Add a dab of glue to help hold the legs in place.

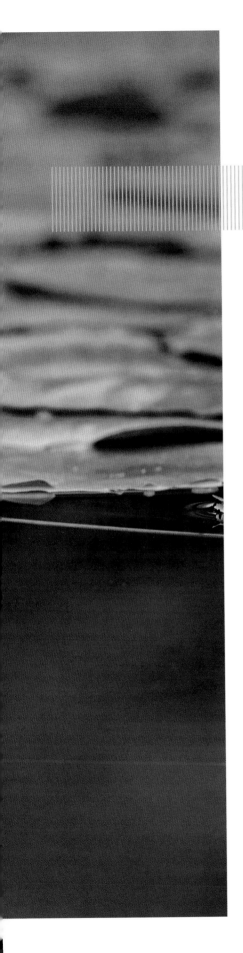

mallard duck

The duck pattern is easily modified to make other water birds. Follow the same pattern using a mixture of brown and tan wool to make a Mrs. Mallard. Use the cygnet pattern on page 39 with yellow or white wool to make ducklings. Include the cygnet and swan, and you have an illustration from the story of "The Ugly Duckling."

MATERIALS

- ⅕ oz. (14 g) white wool
- ³⁄₁₀ oz. (8.5 g) dark green wool
- ⅕ oz. (6 g) gray wool
- small amount of dark brown, black, and gold wool
- felting needle

- foam pad
- scissors
- needle and thread
- black beads for eyes
- ruler

BODY

1. Measure a 7" × 3" (18 × 7.5 cm) piece of white wool roving. Roll tightly into a 2" × 1½" (5 × 4 cm) barrel shape. Needle the surface to help hold the wool in place.

2. Needle one side of the barrel flat. This will be the base of the mallard. Needle one end of the base into a point for the mallard's tail.

3. Needle several layers of white wool to the front to build up the breast. Build and shape the body by adding more white wool to the tail, breast, and back. Needle surface to felt layers together. Finished body measures about 3" (7.5 cm) long and 2" (5 cm) at the widest part.

HEAD AND NECK

4. Measure a 3" × 2" (7.5 × 5 cm) piece of dark green wool and tightly roll into 1" (2.5 cm) oval for the head. Needle the surface to keep it from unrolling.

5. For the neck, measure a 3" × 2" (7.5 × 5 cm) piece of dark green wool and tightly roll into 1" (2.5 cm) barrel shape. Needle the surface and leave fibers loose at the ends.

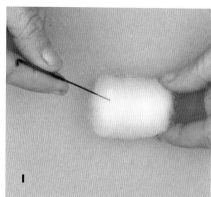

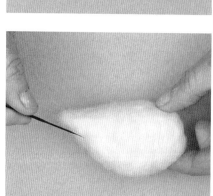

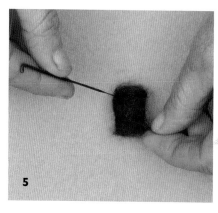

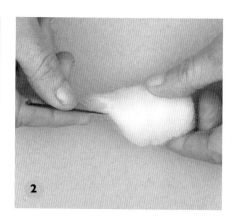

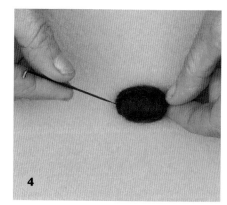

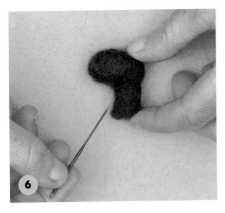

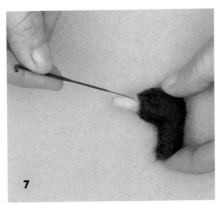

6. Attach the head to the neck.

7. Needle a wisp of gold wool into a small triangle. Position the beak on the front of the mallard's face and needle to attach.

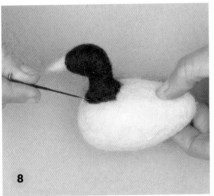

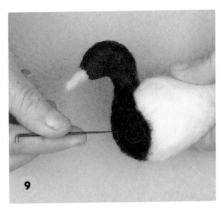

8. Position the head and neck on top of the body and needle to attach. Needle wisps of green wool around the area of attachment to make it look smooth.

9. Needle a patch of brown wool on the mallard's breast.

TAIL

10. Needle a wisp of black wool into a 1" (2.5 cm) square. Needle to the back of the mallard's body.

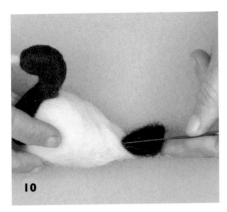

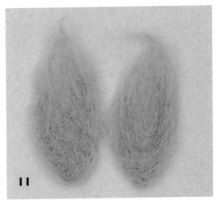

WINGS

11. Measure a 3" × 1½" (7.5 × 4 cm) piece of gray wool. Fold in half and needle the surface flat. Turn the wing over and needle the other side. Use the felting needle to lift the sides toward the middle to form a wing shape. Needle the surface smooth. Make two wings.

12. Position the wing on the side of the mallard's body and needle all around the wing to attach. Repeat with the other wing.

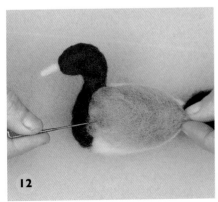

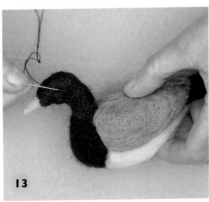

13. Sew black beads on for eyes.

spring chick

This easy pattern will help you gain needle felting confidence and give you a sweet little wool chick that fits right in the palm of your hand. Put a few needle-felted chicks in a basket with some sprouted wheat grass for a charming spring surprise.

MATERIALS

- ½ oz. (14 g) yellow wool roving
- ⅕ oz. (6 g) orange wool roving
- one 12" (30.5 cm) white chenille stem
- wire cutters
- needle-nosed pliers
- foam pad

- scissors
- needle and thread
- black beads for eyes
- ruler
- felting needle
- darning needle

BODY

1. Measure a 5" x 3" (12.5 x 7.5 cm) piece of yellow wool. Roll tightly and shape into a 2" (5 cm)-wide ball. Needle the surface to help hold the fibers in place. Roll the ball around in your hands to help shape it.

HEAD

2. Measure a 3" x 2" (7.5 x 5 cm) long piece of yellow wool. Roll it into a 1" (2.5 cm)-wide ball. Needle the surface. Roll in your hands to make round.

3. Position the head on top of the body and needle to attach. Needle all around the neck area from the head piece into the body piece.

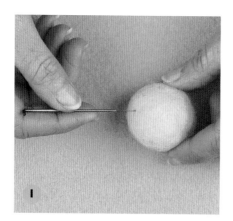

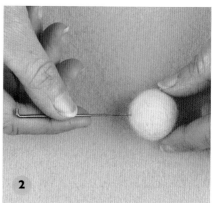

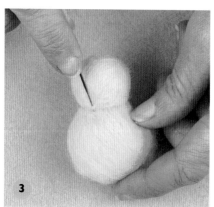

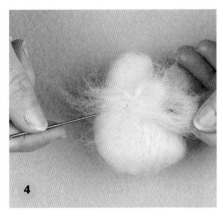

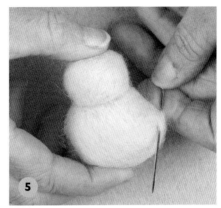

4. Needle a wisp of yellow wool around the neck to help smooth the attachment. Add a layer of yellow wool and needle all over the chick's body and head to help define the shape.

5. Use the darning needle to pull some wool from the back end of the chick to make the tail. Needle to help shape the tail.

WINGS

6. To make wings, measure a 2" (5 cm) piece of yellow wool and fold it in half. Needle into a flat, oval shape. Needle the surface smooth. Turn the wing over and needle the underside. Keep the fibers loose at one end to help attach the wing to the body. Make two wings.

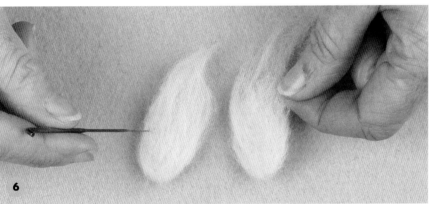

7. Position the wing on the side of the chick's body and needle to attach. Repeat on the opposite side with the other wing. Make sure that the wings are evenly spaced.

(continued)

BEAK AND EYES

8. Fold a wisp of orange wool in a triangle and needle to hold the shape. Keep some of the fibers loose and attach the beak to the front of the chick's face.

9. Thread a needle with black thread and sew it through one side of the head, add a black bead and sew back through the head. Thread another bead on the needle and sew through the head again. Sew the thread through the body and cut.

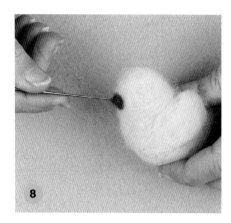

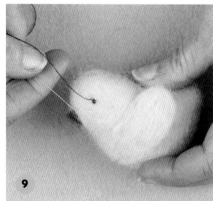

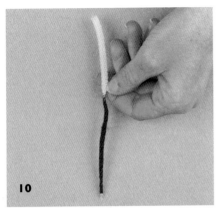

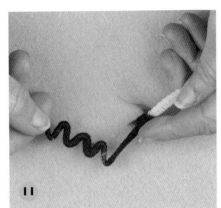

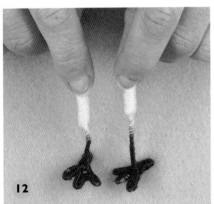

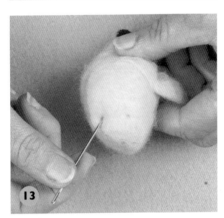

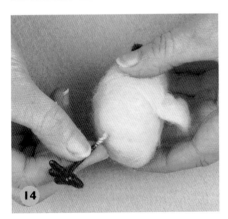

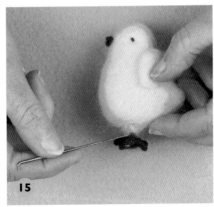

LEGS AND FEET

10. Cut the chenille stem in half. You will be using each half to make one leg and foot piece. Tightly wrap orange wool around half of the stem.

11. Use a pair of pliers to make seven bends in the stem. Pinch the bends to make four claws.

12. Twist the claws to make a foot shape and bend the chenille stem at a right angle to the foot to make the leg piece.

13. Use the darning needle to poke two holes in the wool at the base of the chick where the legs will be inserted.

14. Twist the end of the chenille stem up into the chick's body. Repeat with the opposite leg.

15. Wrap a wisp of yellow wool around the area where the chenille stem meets the body and needle to help fix the leg into place.

love birds

Love birds are made using gray and white wool, but you can choose any color combination that works well together. You can also experiment with needling patterns on the body once you see how fun and easy it is. The possibilities are only limited by your imagination. The instructions are for making the white bird with gray markings. Repeat the same pattern for a gray bird with white markings to complete the pair.

MATERIALS

- ³⁄₁₀ oz. (8.5 g) white wool roving
- ³⁄₁₀ oz. (8.5 g) gray wool roving
- foam pad
- scissors
- needle and thread
- black beads for eyes
- ruler
- felting needle
- two wooden skewers

BODY AND TAIL

1. Measure a 5" × 3" (12.5 × 7.5 cm) piece of white wool. Roll tightly and shape into a 2" (5 cm)-long crescent shape. The middle should be wider than the ends. Needle all over the body to help hold the shape.

2. Choose one end to be the tail and needle it to a flat point. Wrap a wisp of white wool around the tail end and needle to help build up the tail.

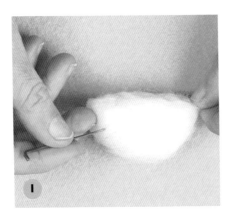

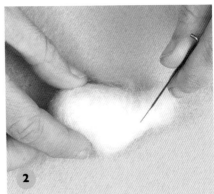

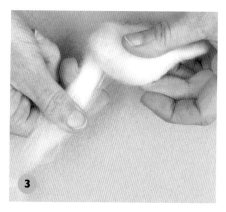

3

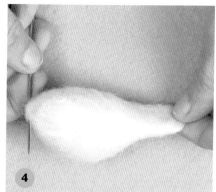

4

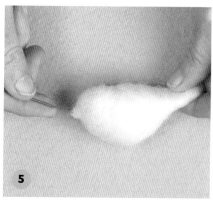

5

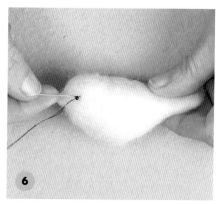

6

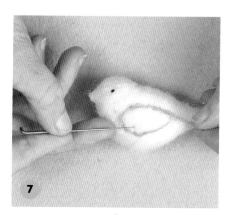

7

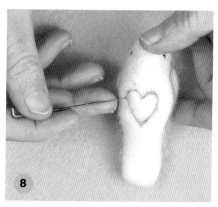

8

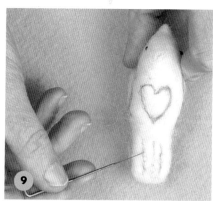

9

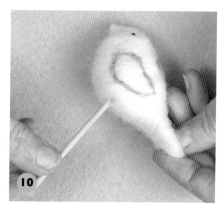

10

HEAD AND EYES

3. The opposite end will be the head of the bird. Wrap layers of white wool around the head end to help build it up and shape it. Continue to add small wisps of white wool all over the body of the bird until you are satisfied with the size. Needle to help hold the shape.

4. Use a darning needle to gently pull loose some white wool from the front of the bird where the beak will be located.

5. Needle the loosened wool into a pointed beak shape.

6. To attach the beads for eyes, thread a needle and pull it from one side of the head through to the other side. Don't pull the thread all the way through. Place a bead on the needle and insert the needle back through the head to the other side. Thread another bead on the needle and sew back through the head again. Sew back and forth a few times to secure the beads to the head.

MARKINGS

7. Using a very thin wisp of gray wool, needle a wing design on each side of the bird's body.

8. Needle a heart shape on the bird's back.

9. Needle three or four lines of gray wool on the bird's tail.

10. To mount the bird on top of a cake, gently twist the wooden skewer into the base of the bird.

bird mobile

These tiny needle-felted birds are made similarly to the larger birds in the book, only on a smaller scale. Choose an attractive branch to hang a collection of tiny needle-felted birds on. Curly willow is good to use for making into a mobile. This is a great gift for a new baby or young child's room.

MATERIALS

- ⅕ oz. (5.5 g) of light blue wool
- ⅕ oz. (5.5 g) yellow wool
- felting needle
- foam pad
- black beads for eyes
- sewing needle
- thread
- fine monofilament thread
- branch

BIRD BODY

1. Measure a 4" × 1" (10 × 2.5 cm) piece of yellow wool roving and roll into a 1" (2.5 cm) barrel shape. Needle to help hold the fibers together.

2. Needle all around each end of the barrel. Roll the piece and needle as you roll so that the whole end is needled down to a point. You should end up with a crescent-shaped body.

3. Gently pull some wool from one end of the body and needle flat. This will be the tail.

4. Needle the opposite end so that it is smooth and rounded.

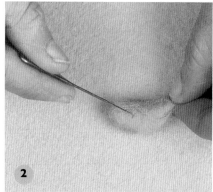

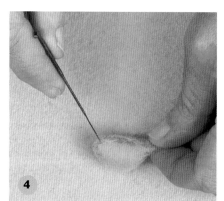

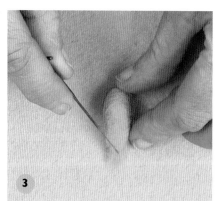

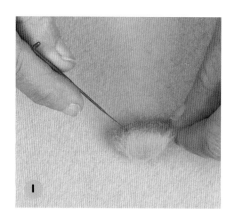

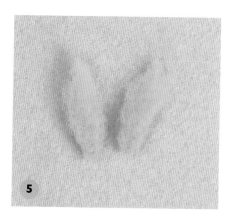

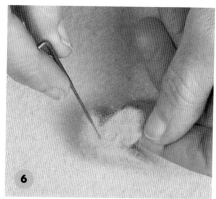

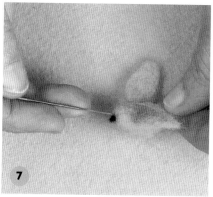

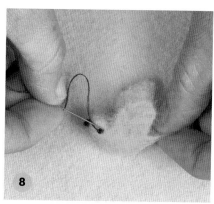

WINGS

5. Needle a wisp of yellow wool into a small wing shape. Make two.

6. Position the wings on each side of the bird's body and needle to attach.

EYES AND BEAK

7. Roll a small wisp of black wool into a ball and needle on the front of the bird for a beak.

8. Sew black beads on each side of the bird's head for eyes.

ASSEMBLE THE MOBILE

9. For each bird, sew a long piece of fine monofilament through the bird's body. Make sure the thread is secure.

10. Attach the monofilament with bird to the branch. Tie the monofilament to the branch and add a little glue to hold in place.

11. Make sure the birds are balanced attractively.

12. Tie a thicker piece of monofilament to the branch to hang it.

bird ornament

This needle-felted wool bird is made to resemble old-fashioned German glass ornaments. You can find the clips in some online shops that specialize in vintage trims. Shiny metallic fiber mixed in with the wool helps to make the bird look festive. Metallic fiber such as Angelina is available in many different metallic colors. All you need to use is a tiny pinch blended in with the main color of wool to make your bird sparkle.

MATERIALS

- ½ oz. (14 g) olive green wool roving
- small amount of yellow wool roving
- foam pad
- scissors
- needle and thread
- black beads for eyes
- ruler
- felting needle
- craft feathers dyed to match the bird
- metallic fiber such as Angelina or Firestar
- clip
- craft glue

1. Before making the bird, prepare the wool by blending it with the metallic fibers. Layer wisps of wool with the metallic fiber and blend together by pulling apart and relayering the fibers.

BODY

2. Measure a 4" × 2" (10 × 5 cm) piece of green wool. Roll tightly and shape into a 3" (7.5 cm)-long crescent shape.

3. Needle all over the body to help hold the shape.

TAIL

4. Choose one end to be the tail and needle it to a flat point.

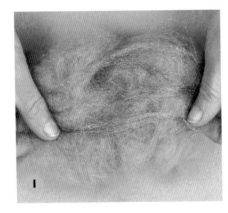
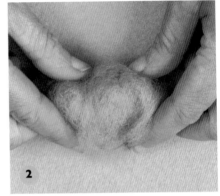
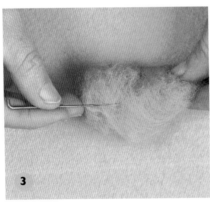
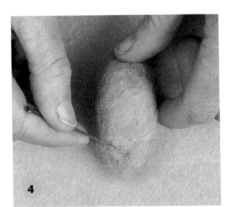

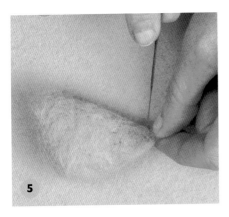

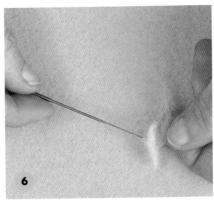

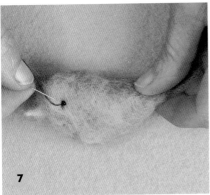

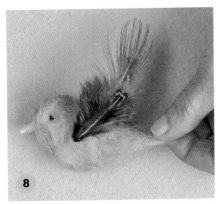

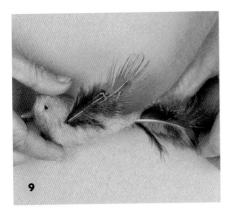

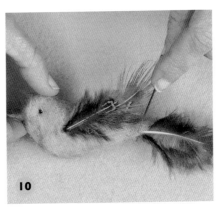

HEAD

5. Wrap layers of green wool around the head end to help build it up and shape it. Needle to help hold the shape.

EYES AND BEAK

6. Needle a wisp of yellow wool into a cone shape. Keep the fibers loose at the wide end of the cone to help attach it to the bird.

7. Position the beak on the bird's face and needle to attach. Sew black beads on each side of the bird's head for eyes.

WINGS AND TAIL

8. Gently twist the end of the feather into the side of the bird's body. Use a small amount of glue to hold the feather in place. Repeat on the other side of the bird. Add more feathers if you want a fuller shape.

9. Position a couple of feathers on the tail end of the bird. Use a little glue to hold the tips in place. Allow the glue to dry.

10. Fold some wool from the tail around the area where the feathers were glued and needle to help hold the shape. Be careful not to needle the glued area; needle around it.

11. Gently twist the clip into the base of the bird. Glue in place.

hummingbird

Small and swift, hummingbirds are truly remarkable. The ruby throat on this needle-felted hummingbird is made using a blend of wool and red metallic fiber, such as Angelina fiber. You can find it at most craft or yarn stores. Copper dyed wool roving can be used instead of green to make a rufous hummingbird.

MATERIALS

- ³/₁₀ oz. (8.5 g) green wool
- small amount of black, white, and red wool
- small amount of red metallic fiber
- felting needle
- foam pad
- ruler
- darning needle
- beads for eyes
- needle and thread
- scissors

BODY

1. Measure a 6" × 2" (15 × 5 cm) piece of green wool. Roll tightly and shape into a 2" (5 cm) shape that is wider at one end and narrow at the other. Needle all over the body to help hold the shape.

TAIL

2. Measure a 2" × 1" (5 × 2.5 cm) piece of green wool and fold in half. Needle the surface to help hold the shape. Leave the fibers loose at one end for attaching to the body.

3. Position the tail on the back of the hummingbird's body and needle the loose fibers from the tail into the body to help form a smooth attachment.

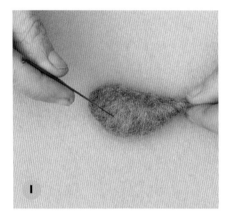

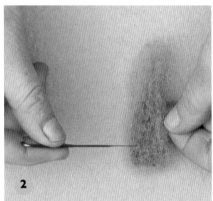

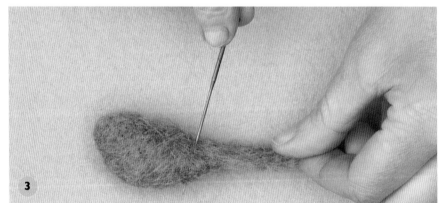

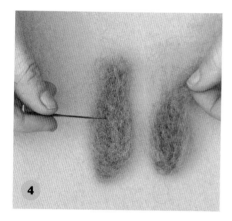

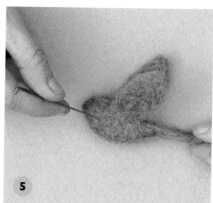

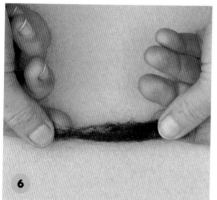

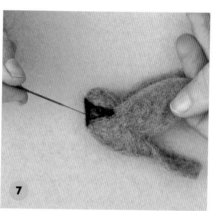

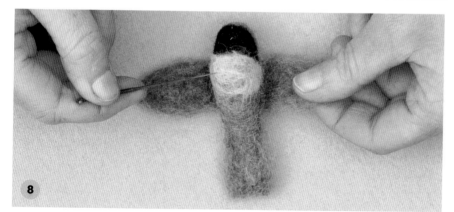

WINGS

4. Fold a wisp of green wool in half and needle to form a wing shape. Repeat to make a second wing.

5. Position the wings on the side of the hummingbird's body and needle to attach.

MARKINGS

6. Use your fingers to blend a pinch of red metallic fiber with a pinch of red wool.

7. Lay the blended fiber on the hummingbird's throat and needle to attach.

8. Lay a few wisps of white wool on the breast of the hummingbird and needle to attach.

(continued)

BEAK AND EYES

9. Thread a darning needle with a thin wisp of black wool. Insert the needle through the back of the hummingbird's head and out through the front for the beak.

10. Don't pull the wool all the way through.

11. Cut off the excess black fiber from the back of the head and needle some green wool to cover the spot.

12. Sew black beads on each side of the hummingbird's head for eyes.

13. Sew a ribbon through the hummingbird's body and give to a friend to enjoy!

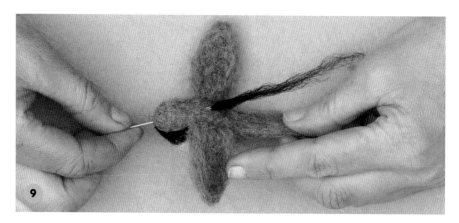

9

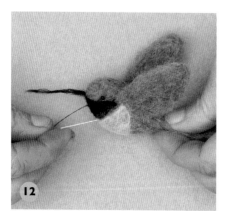

10

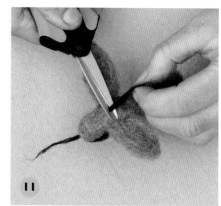

11

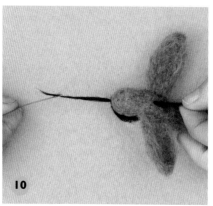

12

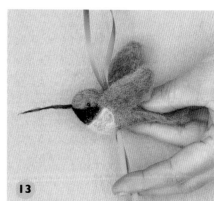

13

steller's jay

Steller's jay is named after the German naturalist Georg Wilhelm Steller, and it's the only crested jay west of the Rocky Mountains. Use a nice, dark blue or indigo dyed wool to make the Steller's jay. You can also blend black and blue wool together to get a darker blue color.

MATERIALS

- ½ oz. (14 g) dark blue wool
- small amount of black and white wool
- chenille stem

- small pliers
- felting needle
- foam pad
- ruler

BODY

1. Measure a 7" × 2" (18 × 5 cm) piece of dark blue wool. Roll tightly and shape into a 2" (5 cm) shape that is wider at one end and narrow at the other. Needle all over the body to help hold the shape.

2. Needle an indentation on one end where the tail will be attached.

TAIL

3. Measure a 2" × 1" (5 × 2.5 cm) piece of dark blue wool and fold in half. Needle the surface to help hold the shape. At the wider end, leave the fibers loose for attaching to the body.

4. Position the tail on the back of the jay's body and needle the loose fibers from the tail into the body to help form a smooth attachment.

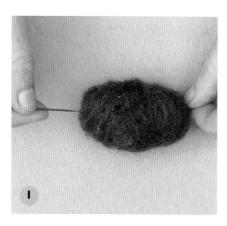
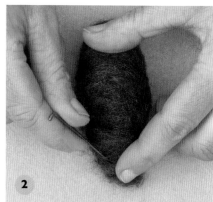
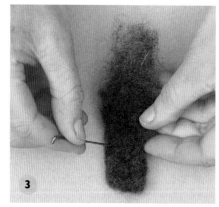
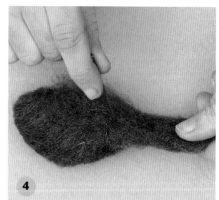

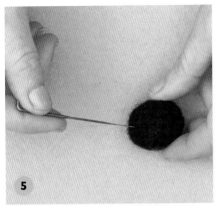

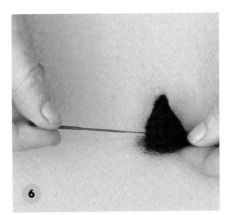

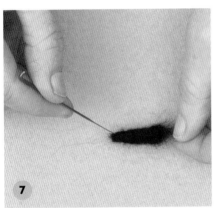

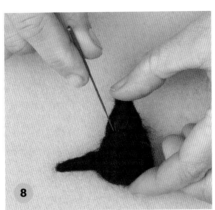

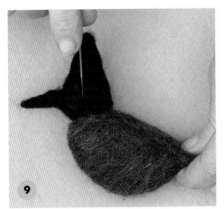

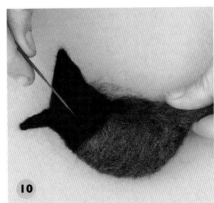

HEAD AND BEAK

5. Roll a piece of black wool into a 1" (2.5 cm)-wide circle. Needle to help hold the shape.

6. Roll a small piece of black wool into a ¼" (6 mm) cone shape for the bird's crest.

7. Roll a small piece of black wool and needle into a very narrow cone shape for the beak.

8. Position the crest on top of the head and the beak on the front. Needle to attach the pieces to the head.

9. Position the head on top of the bird's body and needle to attach.

10. Needle some wisps of black wool around the jay's neck to help form a smooth attachment.

(continued)

11. Gently push the crest back and needle to help hold the shape.

12. Build up the body by wrapping layers of dark blue wool around the bird and needle between layers.

13. Build up the chest area by wrapping with layers of dark blue wool and needling between layers.

14. Needle a wisp of black wool on the breast of the bird.

WINGS

15. Measure a 4" x 2" (10 x 5 cm) piece of dark blue wool and fold into a wing shape. Needle to help form the shape. Make two wings.

16. Position the wings on the side of the bird's body and needle to attach.

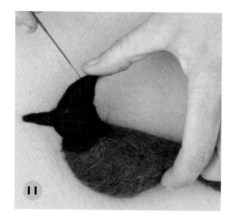

11

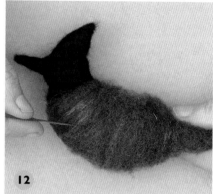

12

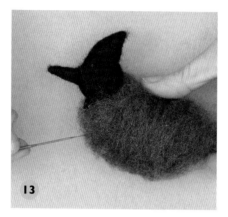

13

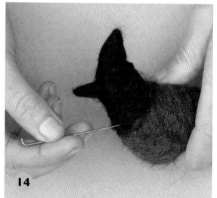

14

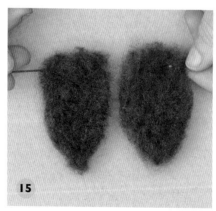

15

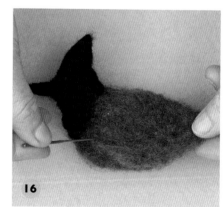

16

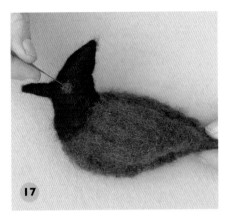

17

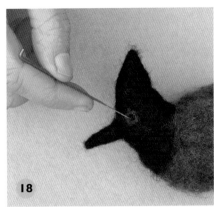

18

19

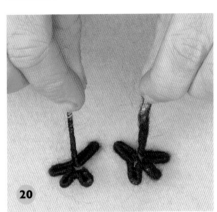

20

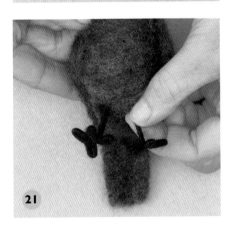

21

EYES

17. Needle a small dark blue circle on each side of the bird's head.

18. Needle a smaller black circle within the blue.

19. Needle a tiny white eyespot on the black circle.

LEGS AND FEET

20. Measure a 6" (15 cm) piece of chenille stem. Cut it in half. Wrap each half with dark blue wool. Using pliers, bend into a claw shape.

21. Twist the legs into the base of the bird's body. Adjust the legs as necessary to help the bird stand.

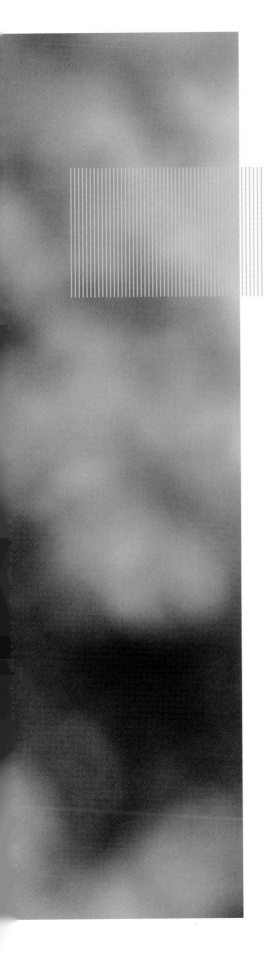

downy woodpecker

The downy woodpecker is the smallest of all woodpeckers. It differs only slightly from the hairy woodpecker, which is just a bit larger. If you want to make more detailed wings with feather patterns, use thin wisps of white wool and add stripes to the wings and tail. Use a decorative looking piece of wood for displaying the woodpecker and attach the bird to the side using tiny pins.

MATERIALS

- ⅕ oz. (6 g) white wool
- small amount of black, gray, and red wool
- chenille stem
- small pliers
- felting needle
- foam pad
- ruler

BODY

1. Measure a 7" × 2" (18 × 5 cm) piece of white wool. Roll tightly and shape into a 2" (5 cm) shape that is wider at one end and narrow at the other. Needle all over the body to help hold the shape.

2. Needle an indentation on the narrow end where the tail will be attached.

HEAD

3. Measure a 2" × 1" (5 × 2.5 cm) piece of white wool and roll into a cone shape. Needle to help hold the shape.

4. Position the head on top of the body and needle to attach.

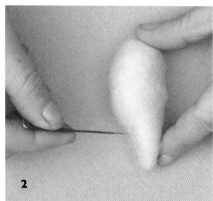

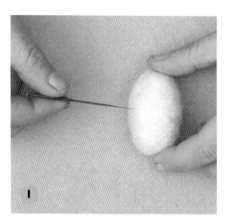

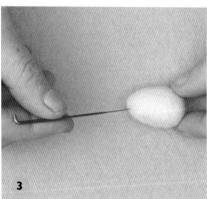

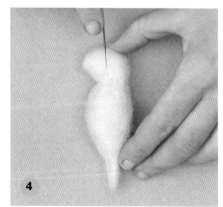

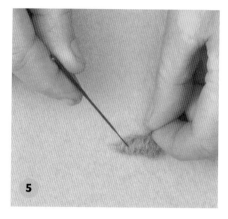

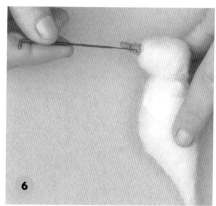

BEAK

5. Roll a piece of gray wool into a ½" (1.5 cm) cone shape. Needle to help hold the shape.

6. Position the beak on the front of the woodpecker's head and needle to attach.

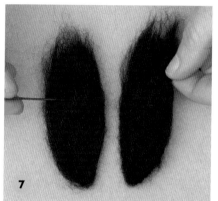

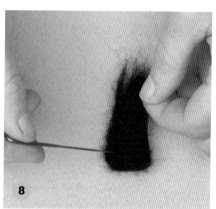

WINGS

7. Fold a 3" (7.5 cm) piece of black wool in half and needle to form a wing shape. Make two wings.

TAIL

8. Fold a 2" (5 cm) piece of black wool in half and needle to form a tail shape. Keep the fibers loose at one end to help attach the tail to the body.

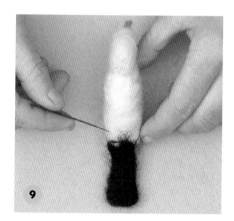

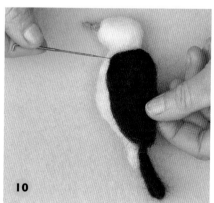

9. Position the tail on the narrow end of the bird's body and needle to attach.

10. Position the wings on each side of the bird's body and needle to attach.

(continued)

HEAD AND FACE MARKINGS

11. Needle a wisp of black wool on the top of the woodpecker's head for a crown.

12. Needle a thin black wisp along the side of the woodpecker's face, near the eye area.

13. Needle a small white circle on the black eye strip.

14. Needle a wisp of black wool on the white circle.

15. Needle a red spot on the back of the woodpecker's head.

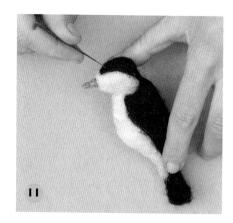

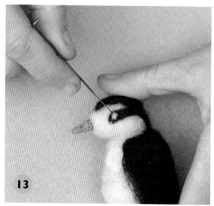

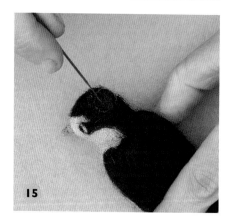

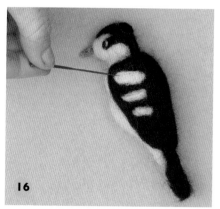

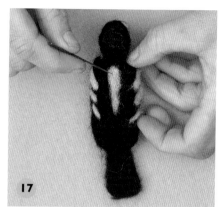

WING MARKINGS

16. Needle wisps of white wool on the woodpecker's wings.

17. Needle a white spot on the back of the woodpecker, between the wings.

LEGS AND FEET

18. Measure a 6" piece of chenille stem. Cut it in half. Wrap each half with gray wool. Using pliers, bend into a claw shape.

19. Twist the legs into the base of the bird's body. Adjust the legs as necessary so that you can attach the woodpecker to a decorative branch.

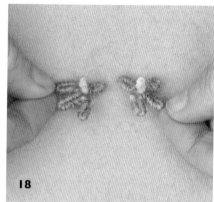

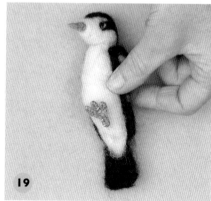

pelican

This pattern is for making a white pelican, but to make a brown pelican instead, substitute brown and gray wool for the white. And if your pelican is hungry, needle felt a tiny fish to put in his mouth. Use a large, decorative seashell as a base to display your pelican.

MATERIALS

- ½ oz. (14 g) white wool
- small amount of black and orange wool
- chenille stem
- small pliers
- beads for eyes
- sewing needle and thread
- felting needle
- foam pad
- ruler

BODY

1. Measure a 3" x 2" (7.5 x 5 cm) piece of white wool. Roll tightly and shape into a 2" (5 cm) shape that is wide at one end and narrow at the other. Needle all over the body to help hold the shape.

2. Needle an indentation on one end where the tail will be attached.

HEAD

3. Measure a 2" x 1" (5 x 2.5 cm) piece of white wool and roll into a ½" (1.5 cm) cone shape. Needle the surface to help hold the shape.

BEAK

4. Roll a wisp of orange wool into a long cone shape. Needle the surface to help hold the shape. Keep the fibers loose at one end to help attach the beak to the head.

5. Position the beak on the front of the bird's head and needle to attach.

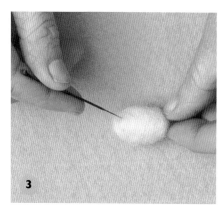

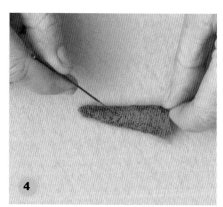

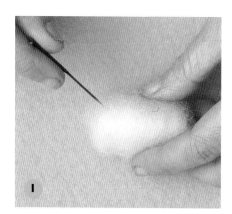

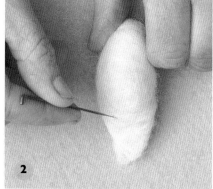

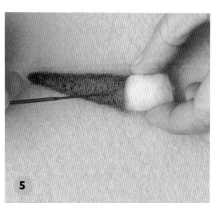

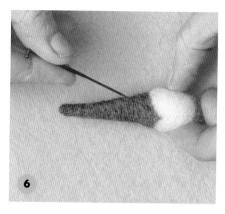

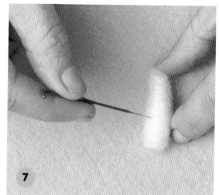

6. Needle all around the beak to help form a smooth attachment.

NECK

7. Roll a small piece of white wool into a 1" (2.5 cm)-long cone.

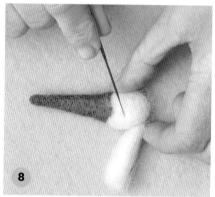

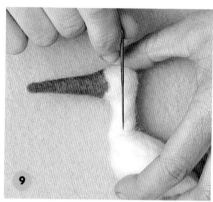

8. Position the head on top of the neck and needle to attach.

9. Position the neck and head on top of the bird's body and needle to attach.

TAIL

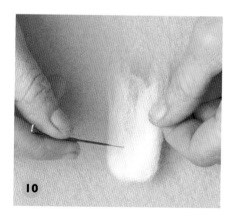

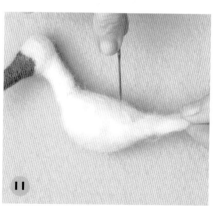

10. Fold a small piece of white wool in half and needle into a 1" (2.5 cm) rectangular shape. Keep the fibers loose at one end to help attach the tail to the body.

11. Position the tail on the back of the bird's body and needle to attach.

12. Build up the chest area by wrapping with layers of white wool and needling between layers.

(continued)

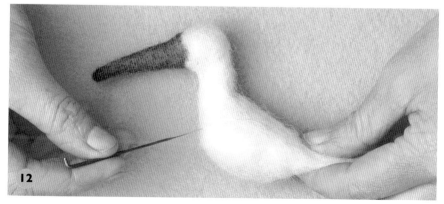

WINGS

13. Measure a 3" (7.5 cm) piece of white wool, fold it in half, and needle to form a 1½" (4 cm) long wing shape. Needle all over the surface to help hold the shape. Make two wings.

14. Needle a wisp of black wool into a small rectangle shape for the wing markings.

15. Needle to attach the black markings onto the base of the wings.

16. Position the wings on the side of the bird's body and needle to attach.

17. Fold the wings over and needle along the bird's back. Add more wool if necessary to help smooth the area of attachment.

EYES

18. Sew black beads on each side of the bird's head for eyes.

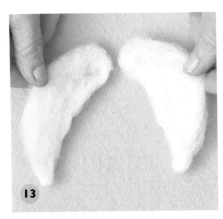

13

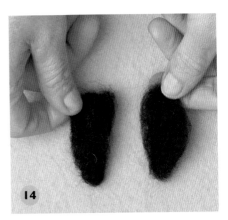

14

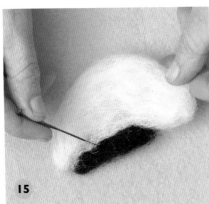

15

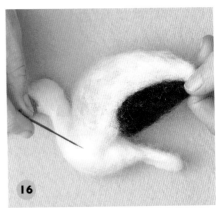

16

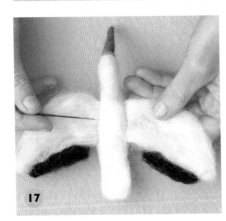

17

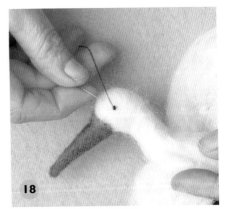

18

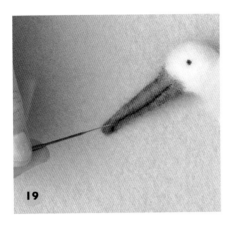

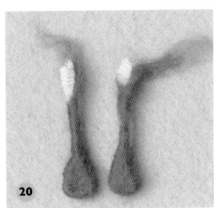

19. Needle a thin wisp of black wool all around the middle of the pelican's beak.

LEGS AND FEET

20. Measure a 6" (15 cm) piece of chenille stem. Cut it in half. Wrap each half with orange wool. Using pliers, bend into a claw shape.

21. Twist the legs into the base of the bird's body. Adjust the legs as necessary to help the bird stand.

22. Wrap the top of the legs with extra white wool and needle to help form a smooth attachment.

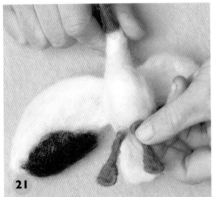

puffin

Oh, there once was a Puffin
Just the shape of a muffin,
And he lived on an island
In the bright blue sea!

—Florence Page Jaques

Puffins are short, chubby, clown-like looking birds with ornate bill and face markings. Make this needle-felted version and give it to a friend who needs some cheering up.

MATERIALS

- ½ oz. (14 g) white wool
- small amount of black, gray, white, and orange wool
- chenille stem
- small pliers
- felting needle
- foam pad
- ruler

BODY

1. Measure a 7" × 2" (18 × 5 cm) piece of white wool. Roll tightly and shape into a 2" (5 cm) shape that is wide at one end and narrow at the other. Needle all over the body to help hold the shape.

HEAD

2. Measure a 2" × 1" (5 × 2.5 cm) piece of white wool and roll into a ½" (1.3 cm)-wide ball.

WINGS

3. Measure a 1" (2.5 cm) piece of black wool and fold it in half. Needle the surface to help form a wing shape. Make two wings.

TAIL

4. Fold a piece of black wool into a ½" (1.3 cm) rectangle. Keep the fibers loose at one end to help attach the tail to the puffin's body. Needle to help hold the shape.

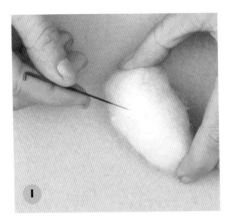

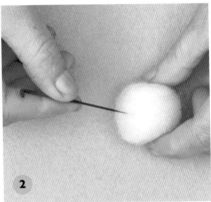

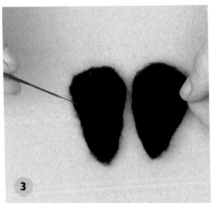

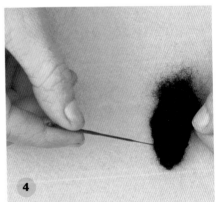

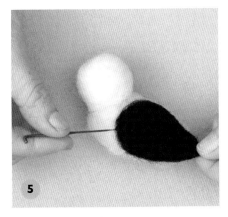

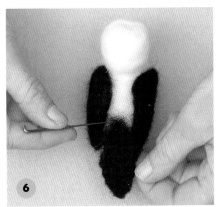

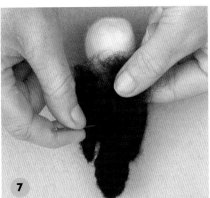

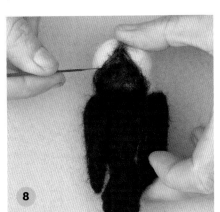

ATTACHING WINGS AND TAIL

5. Position the wings on the side of the puffin and needle to attach.

6. Position the tail on the back of the puffin and needle to attach.

7. Needle a wisp of black wool between the wings.

HEAD, BEAK AND EYES

8. Needle several wisps of black wool on the back of the puffin's head.

9. Needle the black wool so that it covers the puffin's shoulder area and comes around toward the puffin's chin.

(continued)

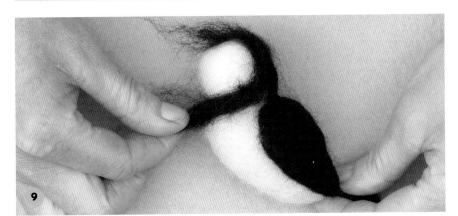

10. Needle the area so that it looks smooth.

11. Roll a small piece of orange wool into a short, wide cone shape. Leave the fibers loose at one end to help attach the beak to the puffin.

12. Position the beak on the front of the puffin's face and needle to attach.

13. Needle a spot of gray wool on each side of the puffin's beak.

14. Needle an orange circle on each side of the puffin's face.

15. Needle a smaller black circle within the orange circle.

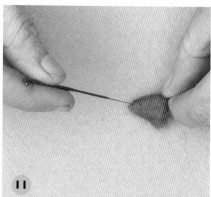

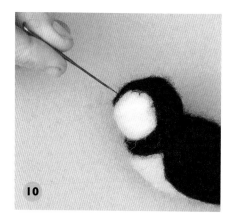

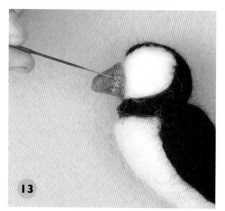

16

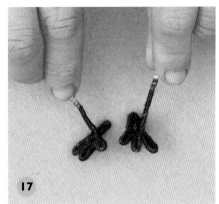

17

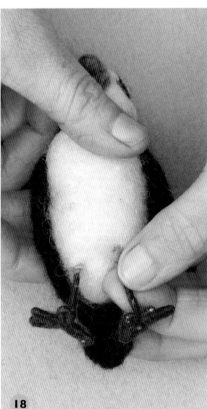

18

16. Needle a strip of black wool along the puffin's eye toward the top of his head, and another strip from the eye toward the back of the puffin's head.

LEGS AND FEET

17. Measure a 6" (15 cm) piece of chenille stem. Cut it in half. Wrap each half with orange wool. Using pliers, bend into a claw shape.

18. Twist the legs into the base of the bird's body. Adjust the legs as necessary to help the bird stand.

gallery

about the author

Since I was very young, I have admired the natural world. The trees have offered comfort, the mountains brought strength, and the sea tranquility. As I grew older, I developed an appreciation and empathy for animals, which profoundly influenced my artwork. I needle felt many types of animals and figures, but sheep and birds appear in my sculptures most often.

Sheep provide me with the raw material for my work, but also with much more. I feel a sense of peace when sitting among my own small flock of sheep. They are amazingly graceful and possess an aura of tranquility; their eyes are big, gentle, and kind. Raw wool fiber is very appealing to me. I love playing with the unusual textures and colors of many different kinds of wool, and it is always an adventure to discover how the fibers will manifest themselves in a project.

I see a hummingbird as a combination of bird, bee, and butterfly. In the Pacific Northwest, hummingbirds are somewhat elusive and it is always a moment of magic when I see one. I am inspired by their iridescence and unique colors. They glisten and sparkle in hues of orange, ruby, green, and violet.

As far back as I can remember, I have enjoyed making things. In the past ten years, needle felting and working with wool have been my greatest passions. I'm inspired by the natural world around our home in the Pacific Northwest, where I live with my husband and business partner, Kevin Sharp. As a professional photographer, Kevin took all the photos for this book, as well as for our first two books together, *Wool Pets* and *Wool Toys & Friends*.

resources

Wool Pets
Laurie and Kevin Sharp
19566 Augusta Ave. N.E.
Suquamish, WA 98392
360-930-0942
www.woolpets.com
Needle felting kits and supplies.

A Child's Dream Come True
1223-D Michigan St.
Sandpoint, ID 83864
www.achildsdream.com
Wool felt fabric and felting supplies.

Joann Fabric and Craft Stores
www.joann.com
Craft supplies and felt. Stores located nationwide.

Michael's Stores
www.michaels.com
Craft supplies and other materials. Nationwide stores.

Magic Cabin
www.magiccabin.com
Craft supplies and wool felt.

Nova Natural Toys
www.novanatural.com
Waldorf-inspired toys, craft supplies, felting kits, and roving.

Weir Dolls and Crafts
www.weirdolls.com
Felting supplies, wool felt, doll- and toy-making kits.

Birgitte Krag Hansen
www.feltmaking.com
Author, artist, and teacher, Birgitte has authored several needle felting books and has a beautiful website full of inspirational images.

FeltCrafts
www.feltcrafts.com
Supplies, kits, and needle felting machines.

Blue Goose Glen
www.bluegooseglen.com
Needle felting supplies, kits, and roving.

Don't miss these other books by Laurie Sharp!

Wool Pets
Laurie Sharp
ISBN: 978-1-58923-525-0

Wool Toys & Friends
Laurie Sharp
ISBN: 978-1-58923-666-0

More books on felting

The Complete Photo Guide to Felting
Ruth Lane
ISBN: 978-1-58923-698-1

Felt Inlays
Nancy Hoerner
ISBN: 978-1-58923-362-1

Felt Fashion
Jenne Giles
ISBN: 978-1-58923-608-5